Life
Is
a
Contact
Sport

KEN KRAGEN WITH JEFFERSON GRAHAM

Life
Is a
Contact
Sport

**Ten Great
Career Strategies
That Work**

WILLIAM MORROW AND COMPANY, INC.
New York

It is the policy of William Morrow and Company, Inc., and its imprints and affiliates, recognizing the importance of preserving what has been written, to print the books we publish on acid-free paper, and we exert our best efforts to that end.

Library of Congress Cataloging-in-Publication Data

Kragen, Kenneth.
  Life is a contact sport : ten great career strategies that work /
Ken Kragen with Jefferson Graham.
      p. cm.
  ISBN 0-688-13282-0
  1. Career development—United States.   2. Success in business—United States.   I. Graham, Jefferson.   II. Title.
HF5382.5.U5K67   1994
650.14—dc20   93-46309
                                                                                        CIP

Printed in the United States of America

First Edition

1 2 3 4 5 6 7 8 9 10

BOOK DESIGN BY PATRICE FODERO

For **Cathy** and **Emma**, the two most important people in my life. And for my late mother, **Billie**, who taught me about the power of giving, and my father, **Adrian**, who has always been my best friend.

ACKNOWLEDGMENTS

I'd like to thank **C. W. Metcalf**, who convinced me that I should do a book, **Mel Berger**, who sold the concept to Morrow, and **Jefferson Graham**, without whose persistence and skills this book, at worst, never would have existed and, at best, would have taken ten times as long to finish. Jeff and I are indebted to our editor, **Adrian Zackheim**, whose belief in our efforts was contagious and who kept us focused on our ultimate objective, and to all the other wonderful people at Morrow, whose enthusiasm for the project encouraged and energized us. I also want to thank my office staff, **Laurel Altman**, **Amy Shachory**, and **Antony Maricevic**, and all the friends who were generous with their time and stories, especially **Jeff Pollack**, **Dennis Holt**, **John Y. Brown**, **Steve Wynn**, **Bob Burton**, **Ralph Destino**, and **Dick Starmann**.

I owe a great deal to clients past and present who have given me back as much as I've given to them, especially **Kenny Rogers**, for twenty-seven years of success, friendship, and fun, and **Travis Tritt** and **Trisha Yearwood**, with whom I have had the opportunity to reapply my strategies and confirm their validity. Finally, to early clients like **the Smothers brothers** and **the Limeliters**, who taught me the business from the ground up, and to the late **Harry Chapin**, who demonstrated to me the power of optimism and opened my eyes to the plight of the hungry and homeless in this country.

Finally to **Aimee Liu** and **Annie Gilbar**, whose earlier efforts never came fully to fruition, but who nevertheless laid a foundation for this project.

CONTENTS

INTRODUCTION

• • • • • • • • •
13

How the strategies in this book have helped turn ideas, causes, and careers into success stories, illustrated with anecdotes and examples from a wide-ranging thirty-five-year career.

STRATEGY I
THE EVENT STRATEGY

• • • • • • • • • • • • • •
19

Here's a way to visualize a career as a series of higher and higher plateaus, and to make upward jumps based on concentrating several events in a very short period of time. This is the key strategy that has worked for so many of my clients, including Kenny Rogers, Lionel Richie, Travis Tritt, and Trisha Yearwood. It is a very simple, yet effective, technique for major career progress.

STRATEGY II
CREATING A PERSONAL BALANCE SHEET

• •
38

How to utilize your assets and eliminate your liabilities on a personal balance sheet, which will lead to a better understanding of what you want to do with your life and your career. This is a critical step in fully utilizing the other strategies in this book.

STRATEGY III
BACKWARD THINKING FOR FORWARD MOTION
• •
52

By thinking backward from your end goal, you can create a road map exactly to where you want to be. Learn how to get the "gatekeepers" (who control access to the things you want) to say "yes" and let you through. Here's one of the most important concepts that will work for you in almost any endeavor.

STRATEGY IV
YOUR LIFE IS NOT YOUR CAREER
• •
69

The idea that your career is your life is a great misconception. The reality is that your career is simply one of the tools you use to lead a better life. Here you will learn to design your career based on your likes and dislikes, and on an honest evaluation of your talents and potential. If you can make the job exciting because you *like* to do it, you're going to be successful and get much more from your life!

STRATEGY V
OPTIMISM AND ENTHUSIASM
• • • • • • • • • • • • • • • • • • • •
79

Optimism and enthusiasm are contagious and real keys to success. They can even help you work your way through the most negative situations. Many actual examples are detailed in this chapter. The principles outlined here work in all aspects of your life, not just your career.

STRATEGY VI
LIFE IS A CONTACT SPORT
• • • • • • • • • • • • • • • • • •
92

You never know just who you'll meet and what future role they might play in your career. A primer on the importance of networking and how to do it, with some great examples from actual careers. You'll be amazed how easy it is to develop a network of important and valuable contacts in your chosen field.

STRATEGY VII
EVERYTHING IN LIFE IS AN OPPORTUNITY
• •
105

Everything that happens in our careers and lives—even the negatives—are opportunities for advancement and success. Here's how to put this valuable lesson into practice. You'll learn from many examples from my career and from those in other areas of society.

STRATEGY VIII
ABSOLUTE HONESTY IS THE BEST GIMMICK
• •
113

There is no better tool for your life or career than honesty. It's a proven technique that will work for you. Best of all, business will beat a path to your door when you establish a reputation for being the most honest person around.

STRATEGY IX
TIMING IS EVERYTHING
• • • • • • • • • • • • • • •
121

There's nothing more critical in timing in careers and life. You can do the best work in the world, but if the timing isn't right, it's going to be wasted. You'll learn how to affect the end results you've obtained by orchestrating the timing of events.

STRATEGY X
THE POWER OF GIVING
• • • • • • • • • • • • • • •
129

The Power of Giving can bring you the greatest rewards in life, not just spiritually, but emotionally and materially as well. You can enhance your life and career by giving to others. This is the chapter where I discuss the creation of "We Are the World" and Hands Across America. How we sold the concepts and convinced forty-five superstars to sing one song and leave their egos at the door—and five and a half million people to hold hands from coast to coast. I'll also show you how these events can teach you invaluable lessons in your own life.

NEGOTIATION
•••••••••
154

Here I explain my approach to negotiating honestly and effectively. How to apply the various other techniques outlined in this book to the important art of negotiation.

PUBLICITY
•••••••
164

I don't care whether you're a milkman, a CEO, or a movie star—everybody can benefit from publicizing their careers. This chapter offers practical advice about how to get it, along with personal anecdotes about my good and bad experiences on the publicity bandwagon during "We are the World" and Hands Across America.

CAREERS
•••••••
176

Here I illustrate why Robin Williams has had one of the greatest show business careers of all time and go on to examine other great careers in business, sports, and politics, explaining how each has survived and thrived by using basic elements of The Event Strategy.

WRAPPING IT UP: WHERE DO YOU GO FROM HERE?
•••••••••••••••••••••••••••••••••••
196

Now that I've explained my ten career strategies, I'll review how now to proceed for success in your own careers.

INTRODUCTION

I made a comment several years ago to *Entertainment Tonight* that has followed me ever since. I was asked this question: "Why does an entertainer need a manager?" After all, a housepainter in Des Moines doesn't have one. "Yes," I said, "but I could take that housepainter and apply the same principles I've applied to the careers of Kenny Rogers and Lionel Richie and make a better career for him."

The next morning, when I came into my office, my secretary told me I had calls from thirty housepainters from Des Moines. That was a wake-up call for me. It made me realize that anyone, regardless of his or her profession, could use the kind of information and advice that I had been giving for years to those in the entertainment business.

Shortly thereafter, I began teaching a course called The Stardom Strategy at UCLA. In the course I show students how my ten principles can be utilized to advance any kind of career. The course is a six-week, eighteen-hour exercise that is time intensive and physically demanding.

I do it because the techniques that I've used to advance careers really work, and I get a great deal of personal satisfaction giving back to young people. When students consistently tell you that the information you gave them has changed their lives, it makes you want to find a way to broaden the scope and get the information out to a larger audience.

Learning from my thirty-five years of experience in the business, from both successes and mistakes, I have formulated several career principles that have worked for me. They can work for you too.

In putting the course together, it took one hundred hours to sit down and think about how to teach what I've been doing for all these years. Why have more than 90 percent of the clients I have represented become major stars? What has worked so consistently? How can it apply to you?

If I can teach these principles to you, I can fulfill one of my life's goals. Hopefully, after reading *Life Is a Contact Sport*, you'll walk away with some tools to have a better life and a better career.

In these pages, I will not only describe how my ten career strategies can be applied to your career. I also hope those housepainters from Des Moines are reading, because I will give detailed tips on how my strategies can be applied to their business—and other non-show business careers—as well.

In the following pages, I lay out my ten strategies and show you how to utilize them in your life and career. I'll also discuss how my past and present clients—a roster that includes Kenny Rogers, Travis Tritt, Trisha Yearwood, Gallagher, Kim Carnes, the J. Geils Band, Lionel Richie, the Smothers brothers, Burt Reynolds, Rich Little, Olivia Newton-John, Harry Anderson, Bill Medley, Pat Paulsen, the Bee Gees, and the late, great Harry Chapin—benefited from them. How, for instance, Kenny Rogers went from being a bass player with The First Edition ("Ruby, Don't Send Your Love to Town") to being an enormously successful singer, actor, and businessman; why Lionel Richie achieved superstardom and then decided to find another manager; why Pat Paulsen's campaign for president was a success, even though he didn't win; how the campaigns for "We Are the World" and Hands Across America were conceived, planned, and executed; as well as my thoughts on some of the more interesting sports, business, political, and show business careers, and how you can learn from their triumphs and failures.

So now you're probably saying, "Fine, but I'm not in show business. How's this Kragen guy going to help me?" Here's the deal:

The principles I talk about are career principles, not entertainment principles.

> **The concept here is that there's a through line to these principles that will work for any form of career. Strip away the trappings of the entertainment business from the things I do, and look at the core of each of the concepts I operate by: advancing a career to another plateau, the use of honesty in all areas of life, the value of optimism, making contacts—none of those things are limited in any way to just the entertainment field.**

The only difference is that in the entertainment business we're generally seeking wider public approval and recognition, and dealing more with mass media. But all of these things can be tailored to fit any career or social interaction.

It is also important to note that it may look like I spend my time dealing just with record companies, booking agents, and the TV networks. In fact, I work closely on behalf of my clients with many of America's top corporations, including Revlon, Chrysler, Kmart, Pepsi, Coca-Cola, Cartier, and Budweiser, to name just a few.

I'd like to begin by telling you a little bit about myself. I own and operate Kragen and Company, a full-service personal management firm. We're a small boutique operation consisting of myself, two secretaries, a receptionist, a runner, and an assistant, handling at this writing just three clients—Kenny Rogers, Travis Tritt, and Trisha Yearwood.

I spend my days and evenings handling the administration, supervision, and guidance of careers. My job is to decide what I will do for my clients, and what they will do for themselves.

From my base as a personal manager, I have expanded into television (executive producer of three series, four mini-series, several TV movies, and numerous specials), politics (as an advisor to the Bill Clinton campaign), and social service ("We Are the World" and Hands Across America).

But primarily, management is my stock in trade. I always say that what a manager does is "everything but sing." In fact, I do everything from coming up with a creative concept for a TV movie such as *The Gambler* for Kenny Rogers to selling the souvenir programs at a concert if the salespeople haven't shown up.

It's whatever is necessary to get the job done for my artists, and that's what makes it so much fun.

I believe that a manager has the second-best job in show business. (Writers are first because everything in this business begins with the written word. Look at many of the successful companies in our field, and most of them were started by writers—Aaron Spelling, Stephen J. Cannell, and Steven Bochco come immediately to mind.) As a manager, you can run your own business and keep your overhead so low you can literally work from your car, provided that you have a cellular phone and a fax in there.

As a manager, you control the access to the talent, and that often puts you in a position to name your role on each project. And let me also add that management is very lucrative. I haven't had a bad year financially since the seventies.

Why do show business performers need managers? Well, like everything else, it grew up as a tradition in the business. In the thirties, there were just agents, but as the agencies began to grow, the agents became so busy with their numerous clients that performers found they weren't getting enough personal attention. An opening was created, and the role of the manager arose to fill it.

As managers became regular fixtures on the entertainment landscape, the agents' work became much more job specific; agents became primarily sellers of talent, rather than overall creative consultants. Also, it became somewhat demeaning and counterproductive for artists to be banging on the door of agencies, record companies, and TV networks, pushing to get things done on their own behalf. It was easier for someone other than the performers to be the one looking out for their best interests and pushing those who needed to do the work for them.

These days a manager is hired to deal with the agents, publicists, lawyers, business managers, and everybody else who gets involved in the performer's career. It might be helpful to compare this to corporate structure: The performer is the chairman of the board, and the manager is the CEO, overseeing all of the departments. Sales is handled by the talent agency; manufacturing is done by the record company, TV network, or movie studio; accounting is the job of the business manager; corporate communications is done by the publicist; the legal department is the lawyer, and so on.

The manager finds himself in the position of keeping all the various "departments" coordinated with each other and making sure they all do their job properly. Meanwhile, the performer can concentrate on what he or she does best: act, sing, entertain, create.

The reason you usually see entertainers with professional entourages is that there is so much business to be done on their career that they couldn't possibly do their shows and take care of everything at the same time. The toll would be too much and their art would suffer.

I view the manager-artist relationship as a true partnership. It's actually like a marriage. Of course, it can have the same kinds of ups and downs as a marriage, but hopefully the same sort of longevity as I have had with Kenny Rogers (twenty-seven years). Sandy Gallin's relationship with Dolly Parton and Irving Fein's with George Burns are two other good examples of manager-client relationships that have lasted much longer than many Hollywood marriages.

Historically, agents have taken 10 percent of earnings, while managers have taken anywhere from ten to 25 percent (with Col. Tom Parker going all the way with Elvis for 50 percent). My fee is generally 15 percent of overall earnings from areas related to entertainment. However, if Kenny Rogers goes out and invests in real estate or chicken restaurants, I don't get a piece of those profits.

You often hear about entertainers making enormous salaries, but once all the commissions are taken care of, their cut is actually much smaller. There's the manager's 15 percent, the agent's 10 percent, the business manager usually takes 5 percent, and sometimes a lawyer also takes 5 percent. So that's 35 percent right off the top. If you've got a touring show like Kenny, Travis Tritt, or Trisha Yearwood, you've also got to factor in the costs of the band, lodging, transportation, sets, wardrobe, lights, and sound equipment, and on and on. Sometimes, there's very little left for the artist, especially after taxes.

Managers get paid well because we have the most important responsibility next to the artist. We're overseeing the entire operation. We're directly or indirectly responsible for all the various career areas that generate income. I always say to my clients that I'll earn a lot more for them than I'll ever cost them, and fortunately, it's always been true. That's how Travis Tritt went from making $20,000 a year before I met him to grossing $5 million two years later; when Kenny

Rogers launched his solo career in the late seventies, he was $65,000 in debt. Kenny hasn't earned less than $10 million a year since.

I can't promise you this book will bring you those sorts of earnings, but I can tell you it will help you to improve your current situation, whatever it is. Turn the pages and begin now to travel down the road to a better, more successful life and career.

THE EVENT
STRATEGY

*My dear sir, the bigger the
humbug, the better the people
will like it.*

—PHINEAS T. BARNUM

On May 25, 1986, five and a half million Americans stood hand in hand from the Atlantic to the Pacific ocean singing "America, the Beautiful," "We Are the World," and the Hands Across America theme song. The 4,152-mile line of people who pledged to help America's homeless and hungry included parents and children, senior citizens, celebrities, several bridal parties, Disneyland characters, native Americans, Catholic nuns, prison inmates, and even some seals and killer whales at Cleveland's Sea World.

To many people it looked like a single history-making moment, but in reality the line itself was at the end of a long series of individual actions and decisions that proved just how powerful coordinated events can be. It dramatized the plight of millions of hungry Americans and sent a clear message to the nation and the government that the time had come to finally address this problem.

It may have seemed that Hands Across America was an isolated stunt, but it wasn't. It was a carefully orchestrated effort, the next logical step in the movement to help relieve world hunger that began in January 1985 when we organized forty-five of the biggest names in music to record "We Are the World." Hands Across America and USA for Africa (the umbrella fund-raising organization that spun out of the song "We Are the World") were both conceived through a process I call The Event Strategy, one component of my ten-step program to turn ideas, causes, and careers into success stories.

No other career strategy reflects the new rules of today's business world more than The Event Strategy. From shipping magnates to used car salesmen, successful professionals all over the world are beginning to use the tactics of politics and show business to build images and increase their personal and professional power. They have discovered that high visibility and momentum can provide the essential competitive edge in any industry; that stardom is as crucial for success in business as it is on stage and screen.

But these are not random or accidental achievements. They are the result of carefully planned and orchestrated events, strategically placed throughout a single career.

> **The Event Strategy is so powerful because it allows you to control the upward progression of your career by making the most of the peaks and plateaus typical of a successful career.**

The basic principle here is that concentrations of three or more events within a short period of time set the stage for major career break-throughs. By event, I mean any out-of-the-ordinary accomplishment that attracts the recognition of your boss, your industry, or the general public.

The first time I realized the power of The Event Strategy was when I began managing the Smothers brothers in the early 1960s. At the time, Tom and Dick Smothers were hardly household names; indeed, they were known mostly to Californians who frequented San Francisco folk clubs like the Purple Onion and the hungry i. But by a fortunate coincidence, I had a deal for a Pontiac TV commercial worth $10,000 (the equivalent of $100,000 today) in my pocket. I was offered the deal with Pontiac on behalf of my clients the Limelighters, who had broken up a few weeks earlier. So instead, I offered the contract to my new clients, Tom and Dick.

Over the next month, they filmed the commercial and were booked as guests on *The Garry Moore Show*, *Ed Sullivan*, and a Judy Garland variety series. By a wonderful stroke of luck, all three shows decided to use these particular programs to kick off their season, and they all ran the same week. Meanwhile, the Pontiac commercial was running every day on the *Today* and *Tonight* shows.

In those days, when the networks commanded over 90 percent of the viewing audience, virtually everyone in the country with a TV had seen the Smothers brothers several times that week. And it showed.

Their next fifty concerts sold out, and TV offers started to pour in. We could have never planned this sequence of events in advance so perfectly, but it worked beautifully and taught me an invaluable lesson. From then on, I became a firm believer in The Event Strategy. I have used it again and again for all of my clients.

> **But even though I choose to work in the entertainment field, The Event Strategy isn't exclusive to just my line of work. It can be utilized for any type of career.**

The normal way to think about careers is to view them as some kind of mountain range that you climb. A traditional climb up the mountain and then a fight to stay at the top.

I don't view careers that way. I think they exist not as a series of mountains and valleys but as a series of higher and higher plateaus which, left unsupported, will erode over time. There can be higher and higher plateaus, but in order to get from one plateau to another, you've got to make a jump, and that jump is based on a series of things happening in a very concentrated period of time—or in other words, The Event Strategy.

You can keep a career plateau from eroding by propping it up with a series of spread-out events, but you won't make the jump from one level to another unless you combine them together in a very short period. The concentrated explosion of activity sends one to a higher plateau. You can keep the erosion to a minimum by a short burst of activity, which will prop up the plateau.

> **What you must do is take a single event in your career or your business life, whether it's something you created or something that happened naturally, and build around it.**

Think of it this way: Imagine that you're seated in a small airplane. You've taken off, you're in the air, and the pilot has given the plane a certain amount of power to get to a particular height. Now he has several options. He can cut the power and glide down to the ground, throw the throttle forward and climb even higher, or occasionally give it a spurt of power to stay at the level he's at.

This is the way I visualize careers, operating just like that small plane. It takes a certain amount of concentrated effort to get off the ground and keep the career propped up, even more energy to get to a higher level.

> **The Event Strategy is an essential tool for any kind of success. It's a way of visualizing a career, and it works much like a scientific principle that you can apply. The key is that you can jump to the next plateau in your career when at least three career events occur in a concentrated period of time.**

I'm a big believer in the magic of threes. So much incoming information competes for our attention that we have to tune most of it out, just to survive. To really make an impression, therefore, we need to be virtually beaten over the head with the information if we are to realize that something big is going on.

It's not just three impressions all from the same source; it's three things coming at you, each from a different direction. For example, think about how you first noticed a new musical group. Perhaps you heard them on the car radio; got home, turned on the TV, and saw a piece on them on *Entertainment Tonight*; then you picked up the paper and read an article. I'll bet it was that third time when you finally became really curious about the group. Where you thought to yourself, They must be hot. I'm seeing them everywhere.

I often say, "I'll give you six events, spread out evenly over two years, and I'll take three of those, concentrate them all in the same week, and I'll be further along in my career at the end of two years than you will be."

In a major show business career, you need two or three events a year to keep an artist from cooling off, to keep that "plane" from starting down. When an artist gets to superstar status, you need to make everything he or she does into some sort of an event so that it represents something special to the audience.

When manager Jerry Weintraub put Frank Sinatra and John Denver together for a concert tour, it was an event that moved Denver's career along significantly. When I talked Kenny Rogers into acting and then produced the first *Gambler* movie for him, it was an important event that is still paying dividends. That's what you've got to do: Keep expanding.

If you're reading this and are not in show business, don't be discouraged. The Event Strategy can be used with *any* career.

The Event Strategy

- How do I make a jump to that higher plateau?
- How do I keep the plateau I'm on from eroding?

Assuming you have the talent and skills, one of the most important things you do to get advancement is to get noticed, to get attention.

So much of our success in life is based on the impression others have of us, be it as a teacher, a boss, a spouse, a parent, or the general public. Single, occasional incidents of good work, good deeds, or public recognition have little impact on these people when the events are spread out over a long period of time. Yet concentrate a few of these in a brief period and you'll be amazed at the results.

In putting together your own Event Strategy, look for big moves. Be innovative. Be daring. Be bold. This doesn't mean that you should perform purely for effect, but it does mean that if you have a choice between working on a project that's been done a million times before and a breakthrough project that's a bit risky, go for the breakthrough. You're more likely to succeed by taking risks than playing it safe.

PERSONALIZING THE EVENT STRATEGY

How can you use The Event Strategy? Well, for starters, you don't have to be a media superstar to make it work for you. Say you're a lawyer, and you want to impress the partners in your firm. Pick a moment when a major project or case you're working on is about to come to a successful conclusion, and combine it with two or three other events, like spearheading the local charity drive, suggesting an improvement in the firm's computer system, or offering a new idea for recruiting law school graduates.

One of my former students, for instance, was working as a recruiter at a large Los Angeles law office, and did such a good job one year that she suddenly found the summer intern program overstocked with so many talented lawyers there wasn't enough office space for them all. So she instituted a pro bono legal aid program, where the young lawyers could gain experience and also make the firm look very good in the public service area. She also solved her space problems, because the work was generally done outside the office.

She attracted attention to herself, and was rewarded for her clever solution with a substantial raise.

Another former student, a secretary hoping to be promoted into management, realized she had to generate events to get ahead. So she suggested that her company hold a food and clothing drive, then volunteered to run it. At the same time, she proposed a slate of new products and programs for development by her division. Soon afterward, she submitted to her supervisor a special report documenting all the ways she could increase efficiency in her department.

These events—one occurring closely after the other—put management on notice that she had the potential to move up, and more important, that she had no intention of remaining where she was.

WHAT MAKES AN EVENT?

There are no hard-and-fast rules about what constitutes an event, but I've found that the most effective ones do have a few common characteristics:

A. *EVENTS ARE SOMETHING SPECIAL OR UNIQUE*

B. *THEY'RE FOUNDED ON REAL SUBSTANCE*

C. *THEY CAPTURE PEOPLE'S IMAGINATION AND ATTENTION*

EVENT *n*: an occurrence, especially when important

Was it really just a strange fluke of nature that *The American Heritage Dictionary*, Third Edition, was somehow able to spend sixteen weeks on *The New York Times* best-seller list in 1992? How did publisher Houghton Mifflin come up with one of the hottest titles of the year, a property that sold over 250,000 copies at the hefty price of forty dollars apiece?

Simple: The company turned the publishing of yet another dictionary into an event.

Good reviews helped. "The most pleasurable dictionary ever published," said *The New York Times*. But Sandra Goroff-Mailly, a Houghton Mifflin promotion manager, didn't stop there. She came up with an innovative marketing campaign that not only relied on the traditional (actor Tony Randall on a toll-free recording discussing different words every week) to the radical—a rap song advertisement that incorporated some of the new words in the dictionary (like *rumbustious*, *shambolic*, and *ethnobotany*).

"We took a nonelitist approach and tried to inject a spirit of fun," Goroff-Mailly told *Advertising Age*. She also got her favorite TV show, *Jeopardy!*, not only to use the new edition of the dictionary as a research source, but also to give away the books to winners, valuable free nightly advertising on TV's number-two rated syndicated show.

Eventful, *adj*: **Full of outstanding events.**

Hear, hear!

MAKING YOUR NEW JOB AN EVENT

The Event Strategy is a very useful tool when you find yourself in a new job, with all eyes looking you over, watching you perform.

First, of course, you must set out to do the job you've been hired to do as well as you possibly know how. But that alone is not usually sufficient. Simply getting the new position is not enough to lift your career to a new level. You need to follow it up with something that's attention getting to announce that you're more than just a new face in the company.

It's critical to make a positive first impression for two reasons: You may not get a chance to make a second one; and it's much more difficult to correct a bad first impression than it is to sustain a good one.

I usually suggest opening with one event, and then waiting a few weeks for the next one. It's important to win the goodwill of your coworkers before drawing additional attention to yourself. Whatever the situation, concentrate on events that make you and everyone around you look good. Enlist the help of coworkers, staff, and superiors so they'll cooperate and dispel the opposition of rivals and naysayers. Here's an example:

A BIRTHDAY BANG

In the 1970s, I worked for super-manager Jerry Weintraub, who at the time handled such clients as John Denver, Neil Diamond, and the Carpenters. I started working for Jerry around the time of his birthday, which is always a great time to do something special for someone. Shortly after I began at his company, I noticed that it was possible to walk into his office, keep on going outside onto his patio, make a circle, and come back in the door again. To me, this setup created only one logical opportunity: a happy birthday marching band!

I traded some consulting work for the UCLA marching band, and got twenty members of the band to come over in full uniform on Jerry's birthday. Unfortunately, at the exact moment I wanted to run the band through his office, Jerry was having a meeting with a rock group he was trying to sign. The UCLA band could stay only so long, so I had to go in there and interrupt the meeting.

I knocked on Jerry's door and said "Excuse me." His face showed that he was quite upset about being bothered. "Hit it, guys!" I said, and with that, the drum major and the band started marching into his office—tubas, drums, trombones, and all.

Jerry lit right up. He was so delighted with this unusual birthday gift that he posed on his balcony for a picture with the band, and hung it proudly in his office for years. (The rock group, by the way, had a great time too, but they didn't sign with Jerry.)

Now there's a situation where I made one of the strongest possible first impressions with my new employer by doing something really unique: creating an event that appealed to the showman in Jerry. I then followed it up quickly with a number of management successes, both in the signing of clients and the handling of clients already represented by the office.

You don't have to go out and hire a local marching band for your first week on the job, but instead you should create your own version of the marching band. It doesn't have to be that demonstrative or flashy either, but it should be unique.

Also be sure the event fits your own institution. For a manager like Jerry Weintraub, a birthday greeting from a marching band was perfectly in synch with the job and personality. It might not suit, say, a conservative establishment like a bank or stock brokerage firm.

Stephen Chao, the former head of Fox News, for example, clearly went a few steps over the line when he hired a male stripper to make a point about morals in society at a 1993 Fox seminar, attended by some very prominent businessmen *and* their wives. His boss, Rupert Murdoch, was outraged, and took Chao outside after the meeting, where he fired him on the spot.

THE ART OF LISTENING

If I was going to work for a new employer now, the first thing I would do is listen and learn as much about everyone there. The more you know about people, the better off you'll be.

Now that I've told you about making your new job an event, I also must warn you to proceed with caution in your earliest days. In many situations, it wouldn't make sense trying to create a series of events in your first week on the job. It could seem like a case of too much, too soon, and get you labeled as a threat to some people, and just plain obnoxious to others. Instead, you should spend the first few weeks researching, finding out who the "gatekeepers" (*see* Strategy III) are who are critical to your advancement, what motivates them, and what their interests are.

Think of yourself as a sponge in those early weeks on the job: Absorb as much as possible. It's not dissimilar to what I do when I get a new client. I don't sign someone up and immediately begin trying to change things. It can take me from two to six months just to get a handle on exactly what I need to do to promote someone's career. The same thing is true of any new job.

Once you know the lay of the land, *then* start planning for a series of concentrated events.

THE MARS PAPERS

I'm a big astronomy buff, and a few years ago I took a course on the subject at UCLA. Once again, I used The Event Strategy to attract the proper amount of attention for my work.

For a class assignment, I wrote what I thought was a very unique paper about Mars, in the style of a travel brochure, promoting a vacation trip to the planet. The day we submitted our papers, I came to class wearing a sweatshirt with a picture of the galaxy. It was an unusual shirt and got a lot of talk in the class.

Then I brought along a letter (it had been hanging on my wall— I collect such rare artifacts) that Albert Einstein had written on the Theory of Relativity. My professor was thrilled to look at it.

The next week, when announcing grades for the class, the instructor said that all the students did really well, but one paper stood out above all the others, and he proceeded to read my paper on Mars.

Now, I don't want to sound like a total suck-up. I love astronomy, had put a lot of effort into the paper, and thought the only way I would ever know what the professor really thought of it was if I got his attention.

You will never get ahead simply by begging for attention if there isn't substance to what you're doing. I wasn't buying grades—I wasn't even taking the course for credit.

> It's just that in today's society, if you've done some really good work, you won't get the attention unless you make that extra effort. There's competition for the attention of your boss, for a date, a raise or a promotion, for a movie role, or even what TV show you turn on. In a free-market, competitive society, attention is simply one of the hardest things to come by, and no matter what level you're at, you have to work at getting it. No one's going to give it to you.

MAKING YOUR BUSINESS AN EVENT

In the past few years, retailers have discovered the benefits of bringing show business-type pizzazz into their stores. The Universal City Walk in Los Angeles, Mall of America in Minneapolis, and Caesars Palace Forum Shops in Las Vegas are all theatrical events. Shopping there is an experience.

The same goes for David Russell's Shoe Carnival, a thirty-nine-store shoe chain based in Evansville, Indiana. "In many of our towns," Russell told a reporter, "we are the Friday night fights and the Saturday matinees."

A visit to Shoe Carnival is like being a contestant on *Let's Make a Deal*. T-shirts are given away to the customers with the most keys on their key chains or for kids who score at the basketball machine; there's a big-toe contest where the shopper with the longest toe gets to grab for cash and coupons blown around inside a glass booth known as the money machine. Managers walk the floor and hand out dollar bills as an apology to customers waiting in long lines.

Russell, who began in Evansville as a salesman for Kinney Shoes and worked his way up to manager, eventually left the firm when Kinney frowned on his wild promotion ideas. So in 1978 he put up $50,000 of his savings and opened his own store. Now he's a public company, sold on the over-the-counter market, and has thirty-nine stores, with plans to open many more.

He made the boring exercise of buying shoes into an event, and customers rewarded him.

On a much larger scale, developer Sheldon Gordon used the same shopping-as-entertainment concept in Las Vegas, where, in the gaudiest, loudest city in the world, no one had ever tried upscale shopping in a theme-park setting.

That is, until Sheldon's $100-million Forum Shops at Caesars Palace opened in 1992. "People are burned out on malls," says Sheldon. "They are looking for something unusual. If you don't give it to them, you will fail."

The Forum Shops are laid out like an elaborate Roman village, with a massive row of arches at the entrance, and fancy fountains and arched facades above each store. Every hour, talking fifteen-foot animatronic statues of Bacchus, Venus, and Apollo come to life for a six-minute show that has shoppers lining up ten to twenty deep.

For many people, shopping is already a prime form of entertainment, and Sheldon Gordon found a way to combine the two. Since he opened, his retail center has pulled in forty thousand visitors a day, ninety thousand on some weekends—three times more than the average shopping mall. All because he found a way to make shopping an event.

THE FREE VEGAS SHOW THAT GOT THE TOWN TALKING

I told you about how The Event Strategy launched Tom and Dick Smothers thanks to a fluke in network scheduling, without my even realizing what was happening at the time. Now let me tell you two instances where I set out to purposely use The Event Strategy to make serious progress in the careers of my clients.

Let's begin by returning again to Las Vegas. It's the late seventies, and Kenny Rogers has just gotten his first solo booking in Vegas. Here's how we turned it into an event and jump-started his solo career.

After The First Edition broke up, Kenny decided to move into his own career as a singer and entertainer. We chose the Golden Nugget, at the time a small downtown hotel, for his debut. I wasn't sure it was the proper venue, as it wasn't as prestigious as playing on the Las Vegas Strip. A bigger problem was that Kenny was booked to play the week before Christmas, traditionally the worst week of the year in Vegas. In fact, in those days, most shows closed down at that time due to a lack of business.

On top of everything else, the room Kenny was to play was a dark, cramped three-hundred-seat lounge. Everything was against us, but we went for it because Steve Wynn, the charismatic owner of the Nugget (he now also owns The Mirage and Treasure Island) loved Kenny, and was willing to work with me to turn this date into a true career event. We also decided that the small size of the showroom was actually an advantage because it would be easier to sell it out.

Still, I wasn't going to leave anything to chance. My task was to motivate everybody—from Kenny and Steve to the Golden Nugget employees, and, of course, the public. We didn't have a lot of money to spend on advertising and promotion, so we cooked up a step-by-step game plan that relied on things we didn't have to buy.

First, we scheduled an extra performance the night before Kenny's opening just for the hotel employees (free of charge, of course). Steve gave everyone free drinks, and Kenny put on a terrific show. The next day we gave all the employees special ribbon badges to wear throughout Kenny's run to encourage them to promote the show. From then on, every time a guest got his baggage carried by a bellhop or his breakfast served by a waitress or his room cleaned by a maid, the guest would see the button with Kenny on it and would hear great reviews of the show from the hotel employee.

Now I had to reach and motivate people who were not guests of the hotel. I decided to approach the local taxi drivers. I went to the dispatching desk of each of the nearby cab companies and gave every driver a flyer inviting him or her and a guest to come to the second show any night free of charge. This would also help to fill the late shows.

Everything worked like a charm. Beginning the next day, all over Las Vegas—out-of-towners coming in from the airport, guests of other hotels, and even local residents were being picked up by cab drivers who raved about the great new Kenny Rogers show at the Golden Nugget.

All this added up to Kenny drawing more people to each performance than the small showroom could accommodate. Lines ran through the hotel and spilled out into the street. Everywhere we went people were talking about Kenny's show and the business he was doing. When this engagement was over, we ran full-page ads in the Las Vegas newspapers with Kenny saying, "Thanks/Sorry. I want to thank the people of Las Vegas who came to the show. And if you couldn't get in, I'm sorry, but as a result of your support, I'll be back for three weeks in May."

It was The Event Strategy that pulled it off—first was the promotion for the cabbies and hotel employees, second was the engagement itself, and the third was the topper—getting Kenny on *The Tonight Show* just before he opened. Within two months, Kenny's first solo hit, "Lucille," was released and he's never looked back.

TRAVIS TRITT AND GRAMMY WEEK, 1993

With Travis Tritt, the goal was to take him from one plateau—as a very popular country singer—to a higher one, where he would be considered for major roles in movies.

It all started when Travis was nominated for a Grammy for his second album. Once that happened, I used every bit of influence and effort in order to get a performance by him on the Grammy telecast.

Ask almost any manager or record company executive and he or she will tell you that the real value of award shows comes from the opportunities they provide for nominated artists to perform. These shows are one of the very few outlets for exposure left on variety television. More important, the exposure often pays off the next day at the record store counter. So once Travis had the nomination, I began trying to make it into a significant event, first by getting the Grammy performance and then building around it.

Next we urged CBS to run the *Rio Diablo* TV movie, which I coproduced, and which starred Travis with Kenny Rogers and Naomi Judd, on the Sunday night following the Grammys. It would be a good move for CBS, because the Grammys were also on CBS and they could use the Grammys to promote the movie. CBS agreed.

Now two events, not just one, were set for the same week.

And there were more coming.

Travis had just done a commercial for Budweiser, but it wasn't scheduled to begin airing until a month after the Grammys. It took some work, but we were able to convince Budweiser that Grammy week was the perfect time to get the commercial on the air.

With that settled, I booked Travis on *The Tonight Show*. This was an event in itself because he had been banned from the show earlier due to my fracas with Helen Kushnick, the former executive producer of the show. This date was his triumphant return.

The idea, of course, was to have all these different things happening in a concentrated period of time (one week, in fact) to create as much public awareness as possible for people who had no idea who Travis Tritt was at that point.

"Travis," I said, "this is a very special week in your life. You will come out at the end of it with a different career than you had before. I'm asking you to work your butt off this week. Do everything you can, be visible and make this thing happen." I don't know exactly how high the events of the week took Travis, but I know it made a difference in every area of his career: records, concerts, *and* acting.

On the Thursday and Friday of that week, I took Travis to meet with movie studio executives, casting directors, and producers. They all said to him, "Everywhere I look this week, I see you. Congratulations on all of your success." Not long afterward, he got a part in a movie with Woody Harrelson and Kiefer Sutherland.

Thanks, no doubt, to The Event Strategy.

LIONEL RICHIE'S ONE-EVENT EVENT

In 1984 we were presented with what was arguably the biggest event of Lionel Richie's career, and got almost no return from it. Very simply, we had done little or nothing to support it. No Event Strategy. I include this here because I believe that showing how something doesn't work demonstrates the theory just as clearly as showing how it does work.

Producer David Wolper saw Lionel Richie perform a rousing rendition of his hit "All Night Long" at a charity benefit. He called me the next day, saying that he had to have Lionel—as the *only* name performer—to close the Los Angeles Olympics with the same song.

His performance during the closing ceremonies was seen by some *four billion people* worldwide. On any scale it was certainly a very significant event, but as I said, there was little or nothing around it to support it. There was no new record album at the time, no major news or magazine stories, his national tour had just ended—and he promptly disappeared back into the studio to record his next album. As a result, there wasn't any movement in Lionel's career.

When I told the story about Lionel and the Olympics at one of my classes, a student raised his hand and said, "Weren't you his manager then? Why didn't you apply your own principles?"

The answer is that sometimes you're so absorbed in the intensity of a project itself and the problems of trying to pull it off that you actually forget how important it is to build other things around it. (Maybe now that I've written this book I'll read it over again before I stage the next event!)

The point was that after the Olympics, Lionel's career didn't advance at all. Had there been other events around the Olympics, he could have reached a higher plateau.

That actually happened five months later. His career got a big boost when he hosted the American Music Awards in January. Lionel stole the evening, singing a terrific version of "All Night Long," and winning six awards.

Then, after the show, he joined forty-five other music superstars to record "We Are the World," which Lionel had cowritten with Michael Jackson. That month he also appeared on the cover of *TV Guide*, released a new album, was written up in the media with major articles, was nominated for an Oscar for his song "Endless Love," and had a new record out that went to number one.

That period was the ultimate career explosion for Lionel. He took a jump to the highest level he had ever reached. He did just about everything you can do in a career in a two-month period. It was one of the greatest convergences of career activities in a short period of time that I've ever seen, and it moved Lionel to a much, much higher plateau.

And all of this might have happened after the Olympics if we had surrounded that event with something.

DELAYING THE EVENT

Timing is crucial with The Event Strategy. If you only have one or two elements together, you might want to put them off until a later date, so they can be coordinated with something happening at another time. The key is that you have one substantive event to build around and at least two others to support it.

Let's say you have a great suggestion concerning an improvement for your company. Unless its implementation is urgent, perhaps you should hold onto it a bit longer until you have something else that you can add to it so that it won't be an isolated idea. Hold the thought to go along with two others, so that they all come together in a fairly concentrated period of time. You'll receive much more attention that way.

I turn down offers for myself and my clients for articles or TV appearances all the time if I don't believe the timing is right. When a major TV show calls about booking one of my clients, the first thing I do is ask myself a question: "What other career things does this tie into?" If I can't find two or three other important things, then I try to delay the appearance to a time when I do have something to coordinate with it.

For example, *The Tonight Show* requested an appearance by Trisha Yearwood in the middle of summer 1993, when she happened to be out on the West Coast for a few days. Trisha and I discussed it, and decided it would be better to make a special trip out West in late October because then she would have a new album, a Disney Channel special, a home video, and a book all out in the marketplace. And *The Tonight Show* didn't mind waiting.

My coauthor, who's a journalist, warns me that if you're a small business, for example, and the local paper wants to do a story on you, they may not be willing to wait for the time when you feel it's exactly right. By that time, the reporter may have forgotten all about you or moved onto other things. My coauthor feels that even if the timing isn't perfect, you've got to jump. My response to that is: If you don't have the bargaining chips and if it's impossible to delay the story, then make the story the central event. Take that opportunity and build around it.

HOW TO MAKE RELATIONSHIPS
AN EVENT

I believe so much in The Event Strategy and the concept of threes that I even use it in personal relationships. Say you're attracted to someone and you want to go out with him or her—obviously you've got to get that person's attention first. You want to get the person thinking about you, and interested, and you do that by making a strong first impression.

Example: You're a student and you're interested in dating a woman in your class. To connect, the first thing you need to do is find out as much as you can about that woman, so you know what her interests are. Then, when you approach her, you have something to talk about, instead of just asking about her astrological sign. If a one-on-one dinner date sounds too threatening, invite her and a girlfriend to have lunch with you.

Once the date is set, immediately go to work on designing your event strategy—look for two or three things that can happen in a con-centrated period of time. Perhaps this sounds a bit too manipulative to you, but the fact is, you're taking charge of the situation. The process is no different in personal relationships than it is in any other part of your life. If you want to be successful at anything, you have to work at it.

If you want to impress someone, you have to do unique things and do more than one of them. For my first date with my wife, Cathy, I picked her up in a 1931 Cadillac. I took her to a special restaurant. I brought her flowers. And I followed up immediately after the date with a note in calligraphy. If you want to make an impression on somebody, it needs to have those beats. It shouldn't just be that one thing. It doesn't need to be extravagant, but it needs to be *special*. And most important it has to say something about you.

That date was the first time I used The Event Strategy with Cathy, but it wasn't the last. Here's another example, when The Event Strategy salvaged what could have been a disastrous Valentine's Day for us.

Recently I had to be out of town on Valentine's Day, which is a night when Cathy and I traditionally have dinner at Chasen's, one of our favorite Beverly Hills restaurants. Valentine's Day is a very important day for us, and she was rather unhappy that I had to be away.

It's hard to be romantic from four thousand miles away, so the first thing I did to make it up to her was to put some personal effort into a gift basket that would be delivered that day with a special card. The key here was that I personally selected the items, so they were things that took a certain amount of thought and showed that I cared.

The second step was sending (the traditional) flowers to the house. Then, before she went to Chasen's that night, to dine with a girlfriend, I called the restaurant, arranged to pay for the meal, and sent champagne to the table with a note.

She called me later that night, in tears, saying how moved she was by what I had done. The flowers were nice, and the basket showed a lot of thought, but it was the third thing that moved her to tears. It proves that The Event Strategy can work in business and personal relationships—providing that the chemistry is right.

Do understand that sometimes you can apply all the principles correctly and you still might not succeed. In human relationships, particularly the romantic kind, there's this mysterious thing called chemistry (I think it's partially based on electrical impulses, but that's a subject for another book), and if the chemistry's not there, despite all the proper planning in the world, you still may strike out. Still, applying these principles gives you the best chance. Good luck.

KEY POINTS

1. LEAPS. Careers exist as a series of higher and higher plateaus which, if left unsupported, will erode over time. In order to get from one plateau to another, you've got to make a jump, and that jump is based on a series of things happening in a very concentrated period of time.

2. JUXTAPOSITION. Concentrating three or more events within a short period of time will set the stage for a major career breakthrough.

3. TIMING. You can keep a career plateau from eroding by propping it up with a series of events. But you won't make the jump from one level to another unless you combine them in a very short period. An event won't service your career in isolation.

4. EXCEPTIONAL. An event is something special or unique that captures people's imagination and attention.

5. PLANNING. In putting together your event, look for big moves. If you have the choice between working on a project that's been done before, or a breakthrough project that's a bit risky, go for the latter. You're more likely to succeed by taking risks than playing it safe.

CREATING A PERSONAL BALANCE SHEET

*It is not much good thinking of a
thing unless you think it out.*

—H. G. WELLS

In the 1970s, I managed the career of a really talented young singer named Dean Scott. He had a huge vocal range and could imitate anybody. He was like Sammy Davis, Jr., in that he could do anything to entertain. The only problem was that, in retrospect, he was probably scared of becoming a star. In any event, he wasted a lot of time trying to be successful.

Every time Dean got to a point where he had to deliver to take the next step, he somehow intentionally failed. If I was bringing important people to watch him perform, he would drop the things from his show that were the most impressive. When I used considerable pull to get him a recording contract, he showed up a week late to the sessions.

Dean had a great amount of talent, but talent alone is not necessarily enough. You also have to have the desire and willingness to step up and deliver at key moments in your career. Really successful entertainers are like Michael Jordan in the last three seconds of a tie game—they want the ball. They know they can score.

I hadn't fully developed an understanding of my management strategies at the time I worked with Dean. I was doing the same things, but pretty much from the seat of my pants. In retrospect, what we should have done was sit down and make a list of his goals and develop a personal balance sheet for him.

He had a great asset, his talent, but also a major liability: *the inability to step up* when it really counted. If we both could have recognized this at the time, we might have done something about it, and Dean could have been a star today. Unfortunately, the last time I saw Dean Scott's name on a marquee, it was a few years ago as I drove by the airport Holiday Inn in Houston.

GOALS

I believe strongly in setting goals to get ahead. The aim is to set realistic and achievable goals rather than grandiose ones that are impossible and will only discourage you.

I set an overall goal first, and then set intermediate goals that are attainable. Such a step-by-step approach will give you the satisfaction of winning when you reach the first goal, and then the next goal will seem closer. The payoff is constant—you win at every little step along the way. I do that, not only in everyday life but also with my clients' careers. (For example, I'll decide to walk on the treadmill for twenty-five minutes, and once I get there, say, "Gee, that wasn't so bad," and keep on going for another fifteen minutes.)

When I embarked on the We Are the World campaign, the task of signing up so many great talents with only four weeks before the scheduled recording session seemed enormous and sometimes insurmountable. So instead of getting up every morning and saying to myself, "Today, I have to sign up thirty of the most famous singers in the world," I created a set of goals to make it easier. I vowed to recruit at least two artists a day until I had the number I believed was the most we could accommodate. And it worked. I did sign up at least two artists every day (sometimes even more), and we eventually ended up with forty-five artists. Then I had to start turning people away.

Setting goals is the very first part of the process of developing a personal balance sheet. When you develop your list of likes and dislikes, assets and liabilities, they will help you evaluate just how realistic your goals are and help you create a plan to accomplish them.

YOUR CAREER LIST

In business a balance sheet is an itemized statement listing the total assets and liabilities of a company at any given time. Based on this information, stockholders decide whether to maintain or withdraw their investments in the business, and upper management determines whether to move forward into new ventures or cut back on existing operations. In short, a current balance sheet reflects the company's immediate past and is used to project the future.

Over a period of time, a series of balance sheets will identify upward or downward trends. A career balance sheet serves exactly the same function. It helps you analyze the assets and liabilities that you bring to your career and use this analysis to develop an organized plan for eliminating the liabilities and enhancing the assets.

I want all of you to now do the same thing I ask of all new clients: Take a few minutes and think about your assets and liabilities, and your likes and dislikes. I believe anyone can best utilize their assets and help to eliminate their liabilities by doing this exercise. The document you produce, in turn, leads to a better understanding of what you want to do with your life and career.

While the ultimate goal of this exercise is to accentuate your positive traits and skills and eliminate your negative ones, I also want you to take a look at your financial assets. Lack of funds may be a liability, while access to funds is obviously a substantial asset. There are numerous examples of people whose financial well-being was the major asset they had to get ahead. Think of Pia Zadora and other performers who critics said "bought their way" to the top. She eventually got her due as a talented singer, but there's no question that her first burst of attention was due to the fact that multimillionaire husband Meshulum Riklis was very creatively financing her career.

THE BALANCE SHEET

Divide a large sheet of paper into four sections: one each for *Likes*, *Dislikes*, *Assets*, and *Liabilities*.

- Under *Likes* simply state everything that brings you pleasure. Think about the things that give you the most enjoyment, whether that's your family, swimming, or going to the movies. Don't just put your job—what is it about your job that you enjoy the most? Working with people or computers, making deals? Back in the seventies, while still single, I placed "playing basketball" on the top of a list of my own and organized many of my activities around my desire to maximize the frequency and level of enjoyment I got from this particular sport. The idea is to maximize those things that give you the greatest pleasure and fulfillment, and minimize those which you enjoy the least.

- For *Dislikes* list the things you least like to do in a separate column. This should be fairly easy. Examples might be, getting up early, being stuck in traffic, building things, public speaking, or whatever.

- Under *Assets* list every positive you bring to your career goals. This includes your financial or material assets, as well as the various kinds of experience you have, your personality traits, outside interests and contacts.

- Under *Liabilities* include not just the material shortcomings, but things such as lack of experience, personality traits that may interfere with your working with other people, as well as fears and hesitations you might have that keep you from achieving your goals.

The answers you come up with will help you determine what kind of career direction you want and determine what tools you have or need to improve. Be ruthlessly honest in all your listings. No one need see this chart but you. Ask someone who knows you well to help you complete this list.

THE BALANCE SHEET

In diagram, your career balance sheet should line up like this example from one of my former students.

Likes	*Dislikes*
Nature	Routine
Exercising	Boredom
Traveling	Obnoxious People
People	Incompetence
Movies	Prejudice
Laughing	Followers
Restaurants	Dishonesty
Music	
Sports	
Change	

Assets	*Liabilities*
Personality	Lack of Patience
Loyalty	Lack of Focus
Honesty	Quickly Bored
Spontaneous	Difficult with Authority
Sense of Humor	Lack of Commitment
Organization	Spontaneous
Confidence	Inarticulate
Creativity	
Independence	
Kindness	

It may be helpful for us to examine the life of the student who created the above list. He is a public relations executive in the entertainment business, in his early forties, married for over twenty years and living in Los Angeles. Bob works out of his house with his wife, representing just three clients—past and present clients have included TV personalities Pat Sajak, Mayim Bialik, and Neil Patrick Harris. Bob doesn't want any more clients because that would give him less free time for traveling. He and his wife love to go to Oregon, where they have a second home.

Bob began in Austin, Texas, managing the careers of young singer-songwriters. He eventually moved to Los Angeles, where he hooked up with a young singer-songwriter named Jude Johnstone. As her manager, Bob did everything from book her dates to handling her publicity. Through this, Bob ended up getting offered a publicist's position at NBC, which he accepted because it was a steady paycheck.

At NBC, he hit it off with *Wheel of Fortune* star Pat Sajak, who asked him to come with him to CBS to handle the PR for his now-canceled late-night talk show. After it was shelved, Pat told Bob that if he ever decided to go out on his own, that he would be Bob's first client. And with that, Bob Burton Entertainment was born.

So now, let's look at Bob's list of likes, dislikes, assets, and liabilities. Let's see if his career services his life. First there are some pretty obvious things. His career appears to allow him the free time and independence to enjoy many of his favorite things: nature, traveling, movies, and restaurants. He also gets to avoid some of his dislikes, like routine and boredom. When you run your own firm, you rarely have time to get bored.

Bob's assets (loyalty, honesty, and sense of humor) certainly are of value in servicing his career. But there are some things on the liability side that perhaps he should be working on to further enhance what he does. I'm specifically thinking of lack of focus, which can be a serious detriment in Bob's line of work or any other. He can probably ignore his dislike of authority because working for himself he doesn't have to deal with corporate bureaucracy. But I find his lack of commitment confusing because it seems he's very committed to the artists he represents. Perhaps there's something behind this that we're not aware of.

Overall, here's a man who appears to have serviced his life with his career pretty doggone well. Your objective should be to do the same.

And here's a *Life Is a Contact Sport* postscript on Bob Burton: He got Jude Johnston a demo deal at A&M Records, though nothing ever came of the record. But he was able to get one of her songs to producer Don Williams, who gave "The Woman Before Me" to Trisha Yearwood for her first album. Jude went on to cowrite Trisha's Revlon commercial song, and has a song on Trisha's third album.

Proof that it's a small world: my coauthor, Jefferson Graham, was going through a list of students' likes and dislikes from my UCLA class, and he randomly pulled out Bob's sheet. I wasn't even aware of the connections until we called Bob.

LEARNING FROM YOUR LIST

So now that you've created your personal balance sheet, where do you go from there? Look at the goals you've written down. Considering the list of likes and dislikes you've made out, are these goals realistic? And if you achieve them, will they enhance the things you like to do, while minimizing those that you don't.

For example, if you don't like to get up early in the morning, your goal of being a Wall Street stockbroker may be something you want to reconsider. On the other hand if, as in the case of Bob Burton, being around nature is one of your major likes, that volunteer work you wanted to do for the Tree People (an organization dedicated to planting more trees) is a natural.

If you're uncomfortable being on television and in front of large groups, and you aspire to write self-help books, you might want to think twice. Instead of writing books, consider other writing opportunities, which don't demand that you go out and promote your work—like screenplays or ghosting speeches for others.

By now, hopefully, you get the idea.

> **What you're aiming for is to use your balance sheet to design a series of goals that are both attainable and will ultimately add to your feelings of happiness and fulfillment.**

You use the list you've created of your assets and liabilities in much the same way. What is it about those assets that can help you achieve what you want, and which of the liabilities need to be attacked?

A great sense of humor doesn't necessarily mean you have to be a stand-up comic, but it could prove a terrific asset in making sales presentations, or a career as a motivational speaker.

If one of your major liabilities is your unwillingness to accept authority, cancel those plans to join the military. However, if you find yourself in a situation where you're happy with your life, but a particular personality trait is holding you back, you may want to approach your friends or even a professional psychologist to help you change your outlook. The key here is that you don't necessarily have to eliminate the liability; what you need to do is recognize it and design your life and your career in a way that you minimize its impact on them. Some liabilities, however, simply can't be avoided and must be dealt with if you're going to be successful.

Lack of finances to invest in your own career is one that immediately comes to mind. We'll discuss this in greater detail in Strategy X: The Power of Giving, but I truly believe that you must find a way to adequately finance the key career moves you'll be making as you move toward success.

Here are some other important aspects or considerations to setting your goals and utilizing your balance sheet.

1. Prioritize Your Goals: Focus.

When we were just beginning to work on Hands Across America, Sergio Zyman, Coca-Cola's head of marketing, came to my office to discuss Coke's role in the event. No sooner had he sat down in my office when he asked, "What are the objectives for this thing? On the back of my office door in Atlanta I have the Coca-Cola business plan so that when someone walks in with a proposal I say, 'See that business plan up there? Does your concept fit in with the objectives of that business plan? If it doesn't, we're not interested.' So what's the business plan for Hands Across America?"

I said, "Sergio, starting today, on the back of my door will be one sentence: FILL THE LINE. That one simple statement is our objective, and we will use it to evaluate every move we make. If we fill the line, we'll be successful. We'll raise both money and demonstrate that the nation wants something done about hunger and homelessness."

Shortly after Sergio's visit, Columbia Pictures, then a Coke subsidiary, offered to give a première benefit for Hands Across America if we would help stage it, get the celebrities there, and sell the tickets. But I declined. I decided it would look good, and get us press, but that the efforts for the première would divert our energy. Thanks to Sergio's question, I saw this as a peripheral effort that would detract from our limited resources and central goal.

Establishing career priorities rescues you from being overwhelmed by too many goals or from getting so caught up in one project that you neglect all the rest. Give priority to those goals that will yield the greatest benefit to you personally and professionally.

2. Tailor Your Goals to Reality.

When I was managing comedian Pat Paulsen during his "presidential campaign" back in the sixties, we arrived for a stop in Kansas City and were immediately surrounded by hundreds of fans. As we stepped off the plane, Pat turned to me and said, "You know, Ken, I think if we really wanted to . . . we could win this thing." Sometimes a fine line separates fantasy from reality. But you have to be able to tell the difference.

Despite the fact that the whole campaign was satire and we went on the air on *The Smothers Brothers Comedy Hour* and asked the public not to vote for Pat, several hundred thousand people still did. So it's understandable why some of this went to Pat's head.

Inevitably, we all have some dreams that are not too feasible. It's perfectly human and probably keeps us young. The secret is to convert those dreams into realistic objectives.

If you're forty years old, twenty pounds overweight and haven't exercised since college, your chances of winning a marathon are somewhat slim. However, if you set your sights instead on reasonable training and conditioning you might finish respectably in a 10-kilometer run. The key is to break down your grandiose dreams into small, realistic goals within your reach.

Narrow your objectives into manageable chunks, then gradually stack them together until you're within range of your ultimate target.

3. Don't Underestimate Your Abilities.

It's very easy to downplay your talents out of modesty; you simply may not realize what your abilities are worth or how they can enhance your career. Here are a few ways:

When you're job hunting, note all of your abilities in your resumé. There was an opening at *Time* magazine recently for an entertainment reporter, and a friend of my coauthor went up against three of the most experienced and hardworking entertainment reporters in town. By all rights, Jeffrey Ressner shouldn't have gotten the job. The two women and one man who were up against him had much more film-reporting experience than he did. But that's the point: *Time* didn't want someone who could just report on film. Jeff also had solid credentials covering music, television, *and* film. Many employers are more interested in someone who can do many things, as opposed to specialists.

Some years ago, a friend of mine convinced me that I should go to a TV-commercial audition Chrysler was having for calligraphers. They wanted a calligrapher to write an invitation to buyers while riding smoothly in the back of one of their new cars. As an amateur calligrapher, I was extremely intimidated when I walked into the reception area at the audition and discovered several of the finest professional calligraphers in town, all sitting there with samples of their work. I immediately dismissed from my mind any possibility of getting this job.

When my turn came, I told the interviewers that I really didn't want the work, as there were several far more qualified people waiting outside to be interviewed. I later learned from my friend that had I not bowed out, I would have gotten the job. They were more interested in a particular physical type than they were in the quality of the calligraphy.

Never assume that your skills or interests somehow make you not right for the job. Often the most creative ideas in business arise out of the least obvious connections.

OVERCOMING LIABILITIES

With a little shrewd maneuvering, you can turn your liabilities into areas of growth. Examine where your skills are lacking and apply the following suggestions to begin building them up:

1. Accept Your Fears.

As I said about my former client Dean Scott, he was simply afraid of success. Because he could neither recognize nor push through his fear, his career disintegrated.

Most of the problems that threaten careers involve some form of fear. Fear of independence. Fear of risk. Fear of responsibility. Fear of failure. Fear of success itself.

The first step toward eliminating such fears is to face up to them and acknowledge all the ways they affect your work. You'll never get over a fear you don't admit you have.

2. Stop Making Excuses.

When my company briefly managed hockey star Wayne Gretzky I suggested he see a hypnotist. But it wasn't to overcome any fear of skating or blades or flying pucks. Flying pucks he could handle better than anybody in the sport.

It was flying airplanes that terrified him. I discovered that Wayne was a true white-knuckle flyer—a fearless athlete terrified of setting foot in an airplane. It was a serious problem for an athlete expected to fly to games with the rest of his team. For a long time he endured the phobia rather than do anything to conquer it. He'd either find some other form of transportation or wreck himself emotionally by suffering through the flight. It took us months, but we eventually got him to stop making excuses and see a hypnotist. Before long he was flying as fearlessly as he skated.

Blaming your fears on circumstances beyond your control does nothing to eliminate them. Let's face it, every career involves circumstances beyond one's control. But you can't expect other people to accommodate you forever, no matter how sympathetic they are. Ultimately, you are the one who has to get off the dime and solve your problems.

3. Commit to Change.

My wife Cathy is a dressage rider and often she used to get nervous before going into a major horse show. After several years of frustration because of this, she made up her mind to get over it. She attended a competitive stress clinic, which helped her focus on the specific issues that made her nervous. She learned to identify her fears one at a time and work through them during practice shows before a friendly audience.

The issue might be a particular riding position or way of handling the horse. It might be concern over the judges or performing in front of the coach. By confronting each problem head on she figured out exactly why she became tense and what she had to do to relieve the tension before it interfered with her performance.

Today her riding has become much more relaxed and professional. For Cathy, as for most people, the hardest part of resolving anxiety is making the commitment to overcome it.

4. Stop Relying on Others.

I used to know a film producer who had never driven a car. When he moved from New York to Los Angeles he found it virtually impossible to conduct business without being able to drive because the city is so spread out.

He soon realized that his career would be in trouble unless he got some wheels, but his solution was to hire a chauffeur most of the time and mooch rides from his friends and associates when his driver was off duty. He pretended he was too busy to learn to drive, but the truth was that he was terrified of the heavy traffic and complicated freeway systems of southern California.

His hang-up was a burden both on himself and the people around him. It took him two years to realize that his phobia overshadowed a large part of his daily life.

To regain his independence he eventually took driving lessons, conquered his fear of freeways, and got a driver's license. He still hires a chauffeur from time to time so he can work while traveling, but he's no longer emotionally dependent on his driver.

5. Admit Your Ignorance.

A president of a large corporation with officers around the globe once told me that the best way to win allies in the business world is to play dumb. As part of his training for the presidency he was put in charge of each of the bureaus for a period of time. Understanding how the business worked in each country meant learning the ins and outs of a different culture, currency system, political context, and social climate as well as the set-up of the office. He found that every time he arrived in a branch office the employees greeted him with suspicion. They expected that the "big boss" would be insensitive and culturally ignorant and turn things around to suit the home office. Well, he was culturally ignorant but not insensitive. He immediately disarmed them by admitting he knew nothing about their routines and re-questing a full briefing before making a single decision. In this way he quickly won their loyalty and managed each office more effectively than he would have done had he bullied them coming in the door.

6. Don't Blame Others.

The world is full of individuals with serious handicaps who neverthe-less carved out astonishing careers. Stevie Wonder refused to allow his blindness to stand in the way of his becoming one of the all-time great singer-composers. Comedian Harry Anderson was dyslexic, but he overcame it to be one of the top stars of television. Mary Tyler Moore and Sylvia Chase are both insulin-dependent diabetics, but their careers haven't suffered because of it. Same goes for Stephen Hawking, the noted astronomer, who both writes and gives lectures despite suffering from a disease that prevents the use of speech. He speaks through a specially built computer.

One of my former UCLA students is a man named Gene Mitchener, whose business card said simply: THE WHEELCHAIR COMIC. What Gene did that was so smart, was to constantly reassess his situation, and see his condition as an asset, not a liability. For example, he once went to a comedy club to audition, and they said, "Sorry, we already have a wheelchair comedian." Faced with rejection one too many times, Gene used his wits and talents to become a successful motivational speaker.

None of these individuals wasted their energy blaming others for their misfortunes. Nor have they used their physical problems as an excuse not to explore new and valuable career skills. Instead, they focused on learning how to overcome their disabilities and got on with their life and work. I know there are plenty of obstacles out there if you're not a white male from a middle-class family. However, it always bothers me when women or minorities use this fact to explain away or accept their personal condition. The facts of discrimination may be true for a group as a whole, but I strongly believe they should never be viewed as a reason for failure by a single individual. That's simply too easy. Too many women and minorities and other disadvantaged people have succeeded in this society by applying sound career principles and taking *advantage* of their situation, rather than hiding behind it. I've often heard Kenny Rogers say, "Those who can, do. Those who can't, bitch."

7. Allow Yourself to Risk Failure.

One of the most common reasons for fear of trying is the specter of failure. Let's say the key managers in your firm all play softball and discuss important decisions during and after practice, but you stay off the team because you're afraid of striking out and dropping fly balls. Accept the fact right now that you'll never be perfect. No one expects you to be. The only way to learn a new skill and get reasonably good at it is to fall on your face a few times and discover what makes one move right and the other wrong. No one will fault you for trying to learn. You cannot think creatively or effectively unless you're willing to make a mistake now and then.

8. Set the Stage Right.

There's a difference between risking failure and setting yourself up to fail. If you're going to take on a new skill make sure you have a fighting chance to succeed. Consider the following factors when selecting the appropriate stage:

- Time: *Are you giving yourself enough time to thoroughly learn the basics of your skill?*

- Tools: *Do you have the resources and equipment you need?*
- Privacy: *Can you practice your new skill as necessary without interference from friends, family, or coworkers?*

Don't forget that even if you've decided that by participating you've set yourself up for failure, you can still play along. If it's a sports game and you're not good at the sport, for instance, why don't you bring along the soda and snacks instead, and be a great cheerleader?

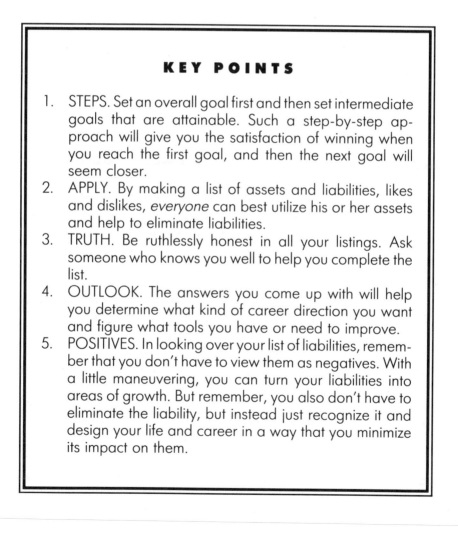

KEY POINTS

1. STEPS. Set an overall goal first and then set intermediate goals that are attainable. Such a step-by-step approach will give you the satisfaction of winning when you reach the first goal, and then the next goal will seem closer.
2. APPLY. By making a list of assets and liabilities, likes and dislikes, *everyone* can best utilize his or her assets and help to eliminate liabilities.
3. TRUTH. Be ruthlessly honest in all your listings. Ask someone who knows you well to help you complete the list.
4. OUTLOOK. The answers you come up with will help you determine what kind of career direction you want and figure what tools you have or need to improve.
5. POSITIVES. In looking over your list of liabilities, remember that you don't have to view them as negatives. With a little maneuvering, you can turn your liabilities into areas of growth. But remember, you also don't have to eliminate the liability, but instead just recognize it and design your life and career in a way that you minimize its impact on them.

BACKWARD THINKING FOR FORWARD MOTION

Losing my virginity was a

career move.

—MADONNA

When my company was larger, employees came to me all the time and said they wanted to move into management. I would say, "Demonstrate to me somehow that you have the qualities to do that job." Handing over an artist to someone for managing is a tricky proposition, because clients are not likely to accept a new person. They want to be managed by whoever signed them.

Harriet Sternberg, who used to work for me as head of my publicity department, moved into management brilliantly. She thought backward from her ultimate goal. She never even asked if I would consider moving her into management. Instead, she went out and signed up two clients: Sheryl Lee Ralph, then an actress in commercials whose star quality was exceptional (she's since costarred in *Designing Women* and *George*) and comedian Harry Anderson in his pre-*Night Court* days when he was still doing his con-man magician act in clubs.

All of a sudden, Harriet *was* a manager. Instead of asking for a promotion, she thought backward. She really impressed me by basically creating a position for herself. Today, Harriet runs her own management company, handling such clients as writer/performer Harry Shearer and parody rock band Spinal Tap.

By thinking *backward* from your ultimate goal, you can create a road map to travel *forward* and get you there. This method can be used to achieve almost any professional or personal goal, whether it's to feed the hungry, design a car, or move into a new position at your company as Harriet did.

> **The purpose of backward thinking is to help you predict at least some of the factors that will influence the decision makers' opinions. The process of backward thinking begins with pinpointing a specific objective and then working backward, figuring out exactly who needs to say yes and what exactly you have to do to get them to say it.**

Most of the progress you make in your life or career is controlled by or subject to decisions made by various people. I call them *gatekeepers* and they must say yes to your plan, your product, your tape, your idea, your manuscript, your desire for employment, even your looks and your personality before they let you pass through the gate.

Backward thinking depends on motivating the gatekeepers who stand between you and your goal. Positioned along the route, each gatekeeper has the power to admit you to the next stage of your plan or hold you back.

Backward thinking starts with your determining or setting an obtainable goal, objective, or destination. Then you work from the goal backward to where you are now, determining the gates or obstacles you'll have to pass through and who controls these gates. Be sure, as you do this, that you *write it all down*. Writing a game plan down is an important part of the process. What you're doing is building a road map from the destination backward to your departure point.

Now how do you get the gatekeepers to say yes? First you must find out as much as possible about what motivates them to open the gate. And the best way to do that is by asking them. Ask for their advice, ask their opinions. Or ask those who deal with them regularly.

If your objective is to get a raise, backward thinking might give you a plan of attack that looks something like this:

- *The Department Head*
  What you need from him or her: an approval of the raise.
  What he or she needs to say yes: a recommendation from your supervisor.

- *Your Supervisor*
  What you need from him or her: a recommendation for a raise.
  What he needs to say yes: evidence that you've increased earnings for your department, or helped save the company more than you're asking. Or perhaps you've convinced them you're invaluable and that other employers think so too, and are interested in hiring you away.

Now let's say you want to star in a movie. The ultimate gatekeeper is the director and/or the producer, whoever makes the final casting decisions. But to even be considered by the director or producer you must be called in to read for them by the film's casting director. And before you get that call, you're going to need a good agent to get you in the casting director's door. And in order to get the agent you're going to need some good credentials. Someone has to give you a job of some kind to give you the experience with which to attract an agent. Perhaps it's the manager of the local theater company. So the process goes.

Now that you have written down your list of who the various gatekeepers are, your next step is to begin to define the things that will influence each of these gatekeepers to say yes to you.

Begin by asking people—if possible the gatekeepers themselves—what influences their decision making. Read the industry books and the trade publications to get a further handle on these decisions and how they are made, and make *careful* notes. Find out from other actors, agents, etc., just what the various gatekeepers on your road map are like and what they're looking for.

Having done a lot of casting myself, I can tell you that in the case of a producer, he or she is probably looking for somebody who can draw people into the theaters or to their TV screen for the key lead roles. In the other parts, the director is undoubtedly looking first for the physical type the role calls for and then for someone with something special he or she can bring to the role.

Once again, write it all down. When you're done you'll have a complete outline to follow forward to the ultimate objective. This works for getting a promotion, making a sale, getting a loan—almost *any* activity.

And don't forget the secretaries, who often hold the key to getting in to see the executive who will make the decision. They too are the gatekeepers.

HOW I USED BACKWARD THINKING TO PUT KENNY ROGERS AND THE FIRST EDITION IN THE FAIR BUSINESS

In the 1970s I was determined to get Kenny Rogers and The First Edition onto the lucrative state-fair circuit. My major obstacle at the time was that most fairs weren't interested in rock groups. So how did I do it? By getting the right message to the gatekeepers.

First I discovered that there were only two hundred fairs that could afford The First Edition's price. Then I determined what was important to them. I found a way to convince a number of those two hundred buyers that The First Edition was not a typical rock group and that they would be a big hit with fair goers.

I began the process by calling several of the country's top fair buyers, agents, and managers to seek advice on how to pursue my plan. They told me what the buyers regularly look for—a conservative, family act that could draw crowds and put on a first-class professional show. I also found out what their objections were likely to be to a group like this.

Next I put together two hundred tailor-made leather-bound portfolios, each one engraved with the words, A PRESENTATION FROM KENNY ROGERS AND THE FIRST EDITION and the buyer's name stamped in gold on the cover. Inside each portfolio was a printed page personally addressed to the individual buyer which read: "Mr. ——, Kenny Rogers and The First Edition are the ideal attraction for the —— State Fair. Here are the reasons why."

On the next page we defused all the anticipated objections to The First Edition: "They are not a hard-rock group." "They are completely reliable." "They are a group that draws from both country and pop fans."

On the following pages were persuasive photographs of the band with people we knew were highly acceptable to the fairs, such as First Lady Pat Nixon (in pre-Watergate days) and key celebrities such as Johnny Cash. There was even a shot of Kenny Rogers mopping the stage at a fair after a thunderstorm.

Finally, we had letters of praise from the five fairs where the group had played in the past. Each letter was printed on the fair's actual stationery so that it looked like an original. The finished product appeared to be tailor-made for just *one* fair buyer even though all the contents were actually duplicates. The total cost of this mailing was $2,500, a sizable expense at the time. But as a result of this campaign, we booked twenty-five state fairs at $10,000 apiece, and made $250,000 that summer. It all happened because I chose to think backward. I identified the gatekeepers, the route I needed to take, and the things I needed to do to make them open the gates.

I should also mention that we worked closely with the late E. O. Stacey, the legendary agent who was The First Edition's representative for fairs at the William Morris Agency. We created a market demand for Stacey to sell into, and then gave him all the credit for the sales.

This brings up another important point: You should never assume an agent or a network or anyone who has lots of other responsibilities is going to concentrate totally on you or your career. Unless you create a lot of heat about what you're doing, to ease the way for the sellers, you're not going to reach full potential results.

STATE FAIR: THE SEQUEL

The next year I wanted to come back even stronger to capture a larger share of the fair business. So I got on the phone and taped interviews with the managers of each of the fairs where The First Edition had played. I asked each manager to tell me his most positive impressions of the group and to pretend that he was speaking directly to another fair buyer who had not seen the band. Then I took these tapes into a recording studio and edited them into an album—which I titled "Sales Hype." Very simply, it allowed the fair managers who were already familiar with The First Edition, to sell my clients to other fair managers who were not. I personally opened the album saying, "I am the manager of Kenny Rogers and The First Edition and I obviously have self-interest here, so you shouldn't believe a word I have to say. Instead, listen to what your fellow fair managers have to say about this group."

On the flip side of the album was a selection of The First Edition's biggest hits and the inner sleeve was covered with the best reviews of their shows. We mailed out two hundred of these records, at a total cost of $5,000, and the result was more than $500,000 worth of fair bookings.

Backward thinking works.

HOW LEE IACOCCA USED BACKWARD THINKING TO SELL THE MUSTANG

Looking for a way to improve his division's sales performance in the mid-1960s, Lee Iacocca, then a vice president of the Ford Motor Company, decided that a bold new car design with mass appeal was the cure.

He began mapping out his strategy by pinpointing the people who would ultimately determine his success or failure: consumers. Researchers told him that the bulk of the market, folks who today would be considered yuppies, were looking for a small, sporty car with a low price tag and lots of style.

Using this information as his starting point, Iacocca worked backward, identifying all the steps and people he'd have to go through to get these customers to place their orders. Here's how Iacocca backtracked from the consumers to the first step in designing a new car:

He knew the only way a consumer would buy a car was via a test drive. And in order to get a potential customer behind the wheel, he'd have to get the car into the dealer's showroom. The way to appeal to dealers was to launch the car with a massive promotional and incentive campaign, which would make the dealers themselves enthusiastic about the new model. On a very practical level, he'd have to get the car built and on the dealer's floor when the marketing push began. To accomplish these two objectives, he would need Ford's marketing and manufacturing people behind him 100 percent.

Iacocca had to convince the marketing people that the car's design had best-seller written all over it before they'd commit. And the manufacturing people needed a design that could be assembled quickly and efficiently using a minimum of labor.

He knew he had the design, but working backward, he realized that it was up to Ford's top execs to allocate the plant, workers, equipment, and supplies to manufacture the prototype.

Once Iacocca had identified all the people who would have to say yes in order for him to reach his goal, he reversed the process and worked forward, beginning with the designers to put his plan into action.

Several months later, Iacocca's Mustang came off the assembly line, and became the car of the sixties, the car that led directly to Iacocca's promotion to vice president of Ford's entire car and truck group, and later on, indirectly became a legendary part of his portfolio when Chrysler, looking for a new chairman, hired him.

USING BACKWARD THINKING AS AN OPPORTUNITY

Some people find that no matter how well they do their job, or how long they've been there, they sometimes can just hit a brick wall in terms of advancement.

Maybe you work in a satellite office, maybe the boss has just stopped noticing you, or whatever. Sometimes if another job isn't on the horizon, the best career solution is to look outside the job for satisfaction.

By thinking backward—how do I get a new job or assignment?— consider taking a part-time night job that could give you more skills that might make you more marketable to your own, or another, employer. Maybe your current boss would think more of you if he or she knew you were also doing some quality work for someone else. Maybe the job you have now would be more enjoyable if you were also doing other things at night, getting an additional creative outlet for yourself.

Jefferson Graham, my coauthor, tells me of the thirteen-week stint he served at *Entertainment Tonight* as a producer-writer, which he has described as the worst job of his career. His problem, coming from print to television, was that he was just uncomfortable working in the different medium. "What kept my sanity," says Jeff, "was the fact that I had cut a deal with the producers up front that allowed me to free-lance for others." So while he worked away at *E.T.* during the day, he began writing articles for *USA Today* at night, which made *E.T.* think more of him. It also had an effect on *USA Today*, which hired him away after his thirteen-week stint at *E.T.* was up.

FOLLOW-THROUGH

In order to keep the gatekeepers on your side after you make the deal, follow-through is essential. Whenever someone gives me his or her support on a project, I express my thanks by writing a personal note in calligraphy rather than a standard business letter, then follow up with periodic notes later on. You can also take the person out to lunch or do something nice for his or her family. If you don't make these kinds of efforts you risk losing the cooperation and respect of the people you depend on; but if you keep the relationship warm, they'll be there to help the next time you need them.

SPENDING MONEY TO MAKE MONEY

John Y. Brown, the former governor of Kentucky and the man who built Kentucky Fried Chicken into a national institution, believes that great ideas will eventually catch on, courtesy of a little trial and error. "Don't ever quit," he says. "There is a final reward at the end."

John Y. got into the chicken business in 1964 when he bought the franchise rights to Col. Harlan Sanders's Kentucky Fried Chicken operation. He bought a recipe and a spokesman, and from those humble beginnings helped to develop the take-home fried chicken business. John Y. sold the company in 1971, got into politics, and then returned to the chicken biz with wife Phyllis George in the 1980s.

By 1991, John Y. was on the fourth version of his new chicken operation. Now called Kenny Rogers Roasters, these restaurants specialize in nonfat, marinated chicken. As of this writing, the company is worth $80 million, and John Y. thinks it will eventually be a billion-dollar enterprise.

From the moment John Y. decided to get back into the chicken business, he was always thinking backward. He knew there was a business in selling tasty, skinless chicken. And he knew that if he could come up with the right way to market it, customers would respond. It was just a question of finding the right recipe.

"I invested in the company by learning everything I needed to know," he says. "You learn more from the mistakes than you do from the successes. We spent several years testing all the different side dishes and different ways to marinate and cut chicken and price it. I had four or five failures before I came up with the right combination.

"Had I quit, I never would have gotten to the finish line. The only test is to let the public tell you what it will take for them to say yes to your product."

John Y. has a perfect "gatekeeper" scenario here. He had to convince the consumer to buy the chicken by coming up with a product the consumer wanted, but he also had to convince potential franchisees that he had a product the consumer wanted, so they would be willing to risk their money to buy a franchise. The third gatekeeper was convincing a corporate spokesman like Kenny Rogers that his credibility wouldn't be undermined by being associated with his product.

SEQUENTIAL FOCUS

One essential element of backward thinking is a tool I call Sequential Focus. It forces you to identify both your long-term objectives and the more immediate goals. You then apply backward thinking to each of these goals in turn.

For example, it's not enough to say that you want to be a CEO by the time you're forty. That's too distant an ambition for backward thinking to work effectively. Instead you have to target specific accomplishments that will become the tactical route carrying you to the top.

What kind of a reputation do you want to establish for yourself? What changes do you want to generate in your company or industry? What specific jobs do you want to experience on the move upward? Where do you want to work and with whom? The answers to these questions provide concrete targets for backward thinking.

With these points in mind, break your long-range career goals into a sequence of focused objectives. For instance, consider these stages for becoming a real estate magnate:

- First, achieve a reputation for good judgment by proving yourself while working for a major local realtor.
- Next, establish your independence by renovating a couple of buildings on your own and getting them showcased in trade journals.

- From this base, begin branching out into larger enterprises, such as shopping centers, office complexes, condominiums, or hotels. It's these last projects that could mark you as a tycoon.

Of course, it's harder in reality than on paper, but the steps and the principle behind them are valid. You cannot expect to build an award-winning shopping mall until you've paid your dues and made your mistakes on smaller projects. That's the purpose of sequential focus.

Back in the days when Kragen and Company was a big company, we had a sports division. Running it was a manager who was great at bringing business in but who couldn't keep the clients because he wasn't doing anything for them. I kept telling him, "Don't go out trying to get any more clients, until we do a good job for the ones we have." If we can deliver for the clients we have, then the rest of the business will beat a path to our door. That's always been my philosophy.

I had a partner in the early sixties, Tom Carroll, who wanted to move to Los Angeles, and I wanted to stay in San Francisco to be away from the sharks. "Those people will eat us up alive," I said. Tom disagreed. "We'll go to L.A. and be unique by being the most honest guys in the business, and that will set us apart," he said. And that's what we did. If you build the reputation, the business will come your way.

The sharper you focus, the better backward thinking will work for you. You'll need fewer people to say yes in order to reach your goal, and the whole process will take less time.

HOW TO GET A HIT RECORD

Again, begin here by thinking backward. Who buys your record and what motivates them to buy it?

In order to get a record purchased, the consumer has to go into a store and find it. But in order for the consumer to want your record, they usually have to hear it on the radio or see a video before making the decision to purchase. And it does no good to get radio or TV to play it if the store doesn't stock the CD or tape.

> ## KEY POINTS
>
> 1. VISION. By thinking backward from your ultimate goal, you can create a road map to travel forward and get you there. This method can be used to achieve almost any professional or personal goal.
> 2. FORETELL. The purpose of backward thinking is to help you predict at least some of the factors that will influence the decision makers' opinion.
> 3. YES-MEN. Most of the progress you make in your life or career is controlled by "gatekeepers" who must say yes to you before they let you pass through the gate.
> 4. PINPOINT. The process of backward thinking begins with pinpointing a specific objective and then working backward, figuring out exactly who needs to say yes and what exactly you have to do to get the gatekeeper to say it.
> 5. CONCLUDING. Backward thinking starts with your determining or setting an obtainable goal, objective, or destination. Then you work from the goal backward to where you are now, determining the gates or obstacles you'll have to pass through and who controls these gates.

The gatekeepers in question here are the radio stations (music director or program director), retail buyers, and video shows.

Think about what it is that makes a radio station program or music director want to play a record:

1. They like the song and/or believe it's a hit.
2. They believe this song fits their format and will enhance the station's success with its listeners.
3. The record is moving up the charts.
4. They think the artist is hot and the public will want to hear him or her.

5. They have a good personal feeling about the artist.

6. They have a strong relationship with the record company, independent promo person, or manager.

7. Research shows the record tests well with their listeners.

8. Their consultant tells them this is a record they should play.

As the radio programmer makes a decision, any one or even all of the factors above may come into play. Clearly, you have to be sure that your product satisfies at least one of these gatekeeper criteria if you're to have any chance at all of getting it on the air. And your odds increase as you fulfill more of these requirements.

What motivates the record-store buyer to stock the record is usually a push by the record company—ads in the trades, a video on CMT, VH1, or MTV, or the actual purchase of floor space. Your record won't sell if it's not in the stores. So you need to begin by motivating your record company to buy the space (all those displays in book, record, and video stores are paid for by the companies!) to get you maximum exposure in the store. One way to do that is to motivate the marketing or sales manager at the record company. We often do that by giving them the feeling that we're in there, working with them every day to promote and sell the record.

I don't know if any of you are aware of this, but one of those housepainters from Des Moines also wants a hit record—he has a garage band that was just signed to Warner Bros. My advice:

- One of the first things he'll have to decide is how badly he wants the music career. I haven't seen anybody make it on a part-time basis. If he wants a music career, and if he's gotten the record deal, he's got to get his business in order to be able to leave it to someone else.

- The next step is to find a good personal manager. That's very important nowadays to record companies. Ideally he should find a manager who has respect in the industry, and who is enthusiastic about his abilities and potential. One who has time to devote to his career.

- With management in place, start working on the gatekeepers—the record company, radio, TV, and retail. Get your music out there, and perform as often as you can to get to the ultimate gatekeeper—the general public.

- What would I say if the housepainter didn't have a record deal or a manager? The best conduit then is a top attorney. In one respect, they're the cheapest person you can hire. Attorneys usually work hourly, or will take a percentage, banking on the future if they believe in you. Even top attorneys take on new clients all the time. I've always recommended that a first-class music attorney can help someone get a good manager or a record deal. They can also see that you're not taken advantage of when you do. It was an attorney who brought me Kenny Rogers and The First Edition back in the 1960s. It was Trisha Yearwood's attorney (followed closely by the president of her record label) who first called me to see if I would be interested in handling her career. Attorneys frequently function as catalysts to put artists and record labels, agents, or managers together.

- The housepainter should also hone his act. When you're discovered, you need to cover as much ground as you possibly can, because timing in the early stages of your career is critical. Be sure you've gained some real performing experience *before* going out on the road.

Take, for instance, the experience of my client Trisha Yearwood, who learned this the hard way.

Trisha was a studio singer who made the jump into a solo career when her former studio friend, Garth Brooks, hit it big. Garth invited Trisha to go on tour with him as his opening act.

She had no stage experience, yet she quickly put a show together. The opportunity was simply too great to miss. First Trisha did a couple of warm-up dates in the Midwest, and then she opened with her first real engagement at the Universal Amphitheater in Los Angeles, in front of the entire industry.

Although the exposure undoubtedly helped Trisha get her career off the ground, the impression she created in those early concerts—that she wasn't much of a live performer—took quite a long time to overcome. She had to work very hard on her show before she became as strong in person as she was in the studio.

HOW TO SELL A MOVIE SCRIPT

Who are the buyers? Movie studios, independent producers, stars, or a TV network. In today's litigious society, virtually none of those people will accept material that doesn't come in from recognized sources. The fact that so many major projects have had suits filed against them, with people saying their scripts were stolen, has made people absolutely wary of accepting anything. Scripts must come from a known agent or another reliable and trustworthy source, or they will almost always be sent back.

The very first thing you have to do is get an agent, or some other well-connected person to act as a conduit. But getting an agent isn't easy. They have lots of established clients whose work they are already trying to sell.

Nevertheless, the world is actually smaller than you think. If you really put your mind to it, you should be able to come up with some people who can make a call or two for you.

Another option is taking an extension course. In Los Angeles and New York, extension classes are taught at major universities like NYU, UCLA (home of my Stardom Strategy class) and USC. Most of the courses are taught by top professionals in the industry, including writers, producers, directors, and others. People go as often as not to meet the instructors or other students and network with them. My class at UCLA has been a wonderful networking opportunity for students.

But speaking of extension classes, this concept exists in every field, not just show business. If you want to be an air traffic controller, somebody, somewhere is teaching a course in aeronautics. Take the course. You'll learn about the craft and unquestionably make great contacts.

HOW TO GET THAT FIRST JOB

There are gatekeepers in every situation. Getting a job in any particular field starts by understanding who the gatekeepers are at the level you want to enter and then trying to find out what motivates them to hire somebody.

Did you make out that list of your assets and liabilities? Well, here's another place for you to utilize it. Let's say you want to get an entry-level job at an advertising agency, as the first step in your goal toward becoming an account executive. To me, the greatest asset you could have is computer skills. So much of what's done in agencies today, from the simple typing of letters to the layout and creation of ads, is done on computers.

If this is the job you're seeking and you have computer skills, great. If they're not up to par, take time before going after this job to improve to a level where you'll impress the people who are doing the hiring at the agency.

On the other hand, maybe you don't know the first thing about computers, but your creative writing skills are strong. What you need to do is to produce samples of your work. Maybe you can even go so far as to take some of the products a particular agency represents and come up with some ad concepts or slogans for them.

Unless your work is truly exceptional, don't expect to walk in the door and get a job as a copywriter or an account executive right off the bat. However, the fact that you've gone to the trouble and taken the initiative to learn something about the agency and its clients, and have created samples of work you might be able to do for them in the future, could possibly land you a job at a lower level at the agency.

> **The point is, don't ever simply walk in the door or go after anything unprepared. If it takes an extra month to do your homework and learn everything you have to know before you apply, take the time. Most likely you're only going to get one shot at a particular opportunity.**

When you go in for your interview, dazzle the employer with your knowledge and ideas. Be prepared to answer questions like: "How would you do the job?" Make it seem like you know the company backwards and forwards.

To get that interview, look at the entire range of contacts you have in your life. There's probably someone who has a contact that will open a door for you. It may even be the waitress at a restaurant you go to or the husband of a friend of yours. It's a question of getting out and asking people. When I want to accomplish something, I tend to talk about it with a lot of different people, and sooner or later I stumble onto somebody who can help. The range of contacts that we have is almost unlimited and most people rarely realize it.

A few years back, my nephew Kevin, who was attending the University of California-Berkeley, knew enough about networking to call his Uncle Ken when he was interested in trying to get a part-time job at George Lucas's Industrial Light and Magic special effects house.

I didn't know anyone there, but I figured it wouldn't hurt to make a call. But first, I wanted to know what particular assets Kevin had that would make him interesting to whoever was doing the hiring. Kevin produced a list, which included his abilities as an artist, his strong musical background, and his credits as a high school student-body president and goalie on the soccer team. These latter two assets might not have direct impact on the work he could do at ILM, but they were sure to impress the person doing the hiring because of his leadership abilities.

Armed with my list of Kevin's assets, I made the call and was pleased to find they were willing to talk to him about a part-time position. And the next thing I knew, Kevin was working afternoons at ILM, gaining considerable experience and having the time of his life.

What did Kevin have to offer ILM? Artistic ability, musical skills, leadership qualities, and youthful enthusiasm. Very often, the thing that you may consider a liability could be one of your strongest assets. For instance, many grads entering the work force for the first time could consider their age a liability. But there are actually many companies, especially those that market products to young people, who search out a youthful point of view.

It's all in the way you look at the situation. Conan O'Brien, a thirty-year-old writer with no TV-performing experience, wanted to host a late-night talk show. Logic says that if he were to make that suggestion to NBC, he would be laughed out of the room. But that's not how O'Brien saw it. NBC needed a new host for *Late Night*, since David Letterman was moving to CBS, and O'Brien convinced network execs that he spoke for the late-night youthful audience that Letterman first developed in 1981. Helping his cause was the urging of mentor Lorne Michaels, the executive producer of *Saturday Night*

Live, who helped discover talent ranging from Chevy Chase and John Belushi to Dana Carvey and Mike Meyers. Michaels thought O'Brien was the right man for the job.

So when NBC announced O'Brien's hiring, he was hailed as the "voice of a new generation." Whether or not NBC made the right choice will be left for the historians, but the fact is that O'Brien didn't let his own career negatives get in the way of going after his dream job.

Take a real good assessment of your own qualities, and whatever they are, treat them as positive assets.

STRATEGY IV
YOUR LIFE IS NOT YOUR CAREER

Who have you ever heard, as
they lay on their deathbed, say,
"Gee, I should have spent more
time on my business"?

—LEE IACOCCA

- *Marilyn Monroe had everything. She was America's favorite sex symbol, a cultural icon, singer, dancer, actress, and star of such mega hits as* The Seven Year Itch, Bus Stop, *and* How to Marry a Millionaire. *But the traditional definition of success wasn't enough to make her happy.*
- *Peter Lynch is someone who also seemingly had it all. After an unprecedented multiyear run, as the stock picker for one of Wall Street's top-performing mutual funds, Fidelity's Magellan, Lynch stunned the investment community when he suddenly announced that he was quitting. He came to the conclusion that his career was not his life.*

For nearly everyone the most important things in life are family and relationships. The idea that your career is your life is a great misconception. Your career is just one of the tools to help you have the most fulfilling and successful life possible.

What are you going to do when you grow up?

That question, which we hear all our lives, preprograms us at a young age for the idea that our careers and lives are somehow synonymous.

The reality is that your career is simply one of the tools you use to lead a better life. I'm sure you've heard this before, but it needs repeating: Find a career you enjoy so much that you'd go to work every day, whether someone paid you for it or not. And be sure that the things the career gives you are the things that will enhance your life.

When I first entered college, I made the classic mistake of majoring in engineering because that was supposed to be the "right" thing to do. It took only a semester for me to realize that I was neither enjoying the work nor doing as well as I knew I could. So I took some career-counseling tests that changed my life. The results showed that I could be an adequate engineer but I would never be very happy or excel at it. I was too outgoing and not organized enough in the ways that an engineer has to be. And my math skills were terrible.

The counselor told me, however, that I did have the personality to be very successful in a profession more oriented toward people than numbers. So I shifted into a combined communications and journalism major and used my college years to groom the talents I needed to launch a successful career instead of an average one.

Today, before I take on any new clients for management, I ask them first to go home, sit and write down what it is that they want to do with their *lives*. To make a list of the things they most enjoy doing—and that they can be anything from sex, basketball, or singing, followed by a list of the things they most dislike doing.

> **What I find so obvious and yet so often overlooked is that you will have the most interesting and successful life if you maximize the things you enjoy doing and minimize the things you dislike.**

If you can make the job exciting because you like to do it, and it gives you so much of what you really want from life, you're going to be successful.

One of my former students was a computer programmer at The Jet Propulsion Laboratory in Pasadena. He told the class that while he loved working with computers, his real passion was music. After he wrote out his likes and dislikes, another student suggested the idea of a career expansion into CD-ROMs, which are now utilizing interactive musical situations. That way, his computer experience would be valuable in an emerging field that also would employ his musical interests.

CAREER DEMANDS

It's important to be very clear and realistic early on about what a specific career goal demands of you. I used to tell my former client Lionel Richie, "Be careful what you wish for—you might get it."

I said that often to Lionel because despite his warm, accessible image, he is a very private person and wasn't always comfortable being a public figure. To a certain extent, all of those demands of career success and that constant need to better the last album and the last tour, to be bigger and more successful, would weigh heavily on him. It was hard for him to deal with the concept of not being able to top himself each time out.

Like sitcom actors, who want to be movie stars, and movie stars, who want to be critically acclaimed on Broadway, Lionel wanted a different kind of career from the one he had. He was a genius at crafting commercial pop tunes that would sell millions of records, but got somewhat limited critical acclaim. His music, like his image, was open and accessible, and his outward personality was warm and entertaining and charming. Suddenly, however, he wanted to be more like Prince, Bruce Springsteen, or Michael Jackson.

I'm not saying you shouldn't try to stretch, but you should also be realistic about your strengths and weaknesses. Everybody has his or her own uniqueness. Trying to be something you're not suited for is a mistake I see time and time again.

THE ART OF THE DECLINE

> One thing I do before adding a new client or project is to ask myself: "What does this *add* to my life that I really need or want?" You don't have to be at my level or stage in life to use this principle. It can be used anytime.

Say you're a junior executive at an accounting firm, and you're offered a lateral move at another company, one that will increase your work load 30 percent and pay 10 percent. Is it worth it to make the move? Will your life be a happier one? It's a real short life, and you've got to focus on getting the most out of it. How important is that 10 percent? How much will it be after taxes? Will you have time to do anything with the extra money?

You can use this tool in evaluating any new opportunity that comes your way. In my life, I've finally learned to say no! I turn down clients every week because three feels like all I can handle. Every time I think of adding a new client, I first ask myself if my life would be better with another client in it. Do I need more money, excitement, challenges? Or could the time spent with a new client be used to do a better job for the clients I already have? Sure, additional clients would give me more security, but doing the best job for the clients I already have in the long run produces the greatest job security of all.

At this stage in my life, the one thing I long for more than anything else is free time. It's rare that any project you take on can give you more time. Would a new client help me achieve that goal? Probably not.

But will it challenge me to do something I've never done? Will it be so much fun that I'll have a great time doing it? Those are good questions to ask as well.

With Travis Tritt it was: "Can I still do this?" Can I still start from scratch and break a new career? Then with Trisha Yearwood, I had already established this network of country relationships and contacts, and she could benefit from that. Plus, I could see an immediate game plan. She had so much untapped potential, and we had so much personal rapport.

OK, so why did I decide to spend all the hours putting this book together—how did *that* improve my life?

Almost every day, someone asks me for career advice. If I'm not currently teaching my course at UCLA, the only thing I can offer is a series of tapes, which were recorded and edited the first year I taught. But since that initial year I have constantly improved my teaching techniques and have learned a great deal from my students.

I've continued, however, to feel the need to say to somebody, "Here is what I know and how to do it. Read it and learn for yourself from my experiences."

So yes, writing the book does rob me of free time now, but there's a long-term value in it—it will save me time in the future when people ask me for advice. And even better, as you can read in Strategy X— giving back is one of the most satisfying things in life.

OUTSIDE INTERESTS

I feel that the most important things in life are these:

1. *Physical well-being* (eating well, staying healthy)
2. *Social relationships* (family and friends)
3. *Careers*
4. *Outside interests* (hobbies, charity work, playing or watching sports, etc.)

In my life I put a lot of emphasis on physical exercise. I believe it's a great counter to depression, something that gives you a lot of energy to deal with things during the day.

A few years ago I had lunch with a director friend of mine who told me he was so depressed that he couldn't get out of bed in the morning. He had just turned fifty, hadn't worked in a while, and felt his career was over.

"Wait," I said, "let's look at your situation. What do you have the most of right now? Free time. What if you took an hour or two a day, and went for a good long walk? It might help you get over your depression. If you can get over that, a lot of things will begin to turn around for you."

Several months later, I called him to see how he was doing. "You won't believe this," he told me, "but I started walking, and then graduated to jogging and I started feeling terrific. I lost weight, and guess what—I just went back to work." I believe the change in attitude is what did it. I always try to find something to break the cycle, and at the very least, exercise is always a positive step in the right direction.

I start my business day every day with either a workout in the gym, or by heading over to UCLA to play basketball with a group of guys I've been playing with for several years. The terrific thing about basketball is that I've never once in my life thought about anything on the court except getting the ball into the hoop. I can't say the same for swimming, jogging, or other solo sports. With them, my mind is awash in business, and I'm a big believer in stepping back from the grind. That's one of the things that's kept me going all these years.

After B-ball or a workout at home, I begin working the phone.

GROWING TO SUCCEED

At one point in the 1980s, I got swept up by the success thing, and added employees and divisions left and right. I wasn't practicing what I preached. I've always said that your career ought to service your life, but my career wasn't servicing my life. It was servicing some misconception that I had learned from society that said size was all important.

Instead, I spent most of the time worrying about how to meet a monthly $200,000 payroll and being responsible for fifty employees, and apologizing to clients who thought they would be getting my personal services but instead ended up with some of my staffers.

Then one of the most powerful men in Hollywood did me a big favor. Merv Adelson was running Lorimar Productions in the 1980s before it was bought by Time Warner. For a time, Merv was on quite a shopping spree. He bought the Bozell advertising agency and Bernie Brillstein's management company. Now he wanted to buy Kragen and Company. We had serious talks, and we almost made a $15-million deal until one of Hollywood's top talent agents killed it. The agent was worried that with a studio owning two management firms, somehow the agents would get squeezed out. And he threatened not to let any of his clients do business with Lorimar. So Merv understandably got cold feet.

So I didn't sell my company. In retrospect, that was one of the greatest favors anybody has ever done for me. Even though I was pretty charged up about selling to Lorimar, I came to realize that my own satisfaction was based on the freedom to work for myself—not having to answer to anybody but my clients. I get to reap the fruits of my own labors, and I don't go to work and compete with a guy sitting in the next cubicle.

> **There is an enormous human drive to grow, to get bigger, to be the biggest kid on your block. Success is somehow equated with the size of the institution in society, but size is very often self-defeating. Larger companies aren't necessarily happier places to work than small companies, even though there's something intoxicating about size. You get swept up in that euphoric feeling, and you lose sight of what it is that is really going to give you the most enjoyment.**

COMING TO TERMS WITH WHAT MAKES YOU HAPPY

Jim Patterson was on the West Coast shooting a series of Burger King TV commercials for his employer, the New York ad agency J. Walter Thompson, when he got news that his latest novel, *Virgin*, had been sold to the movies and all the major book clubs. Patterson had written several successful books before, but none had hit the big time like this.

You'd think he'd have been elated, but he wasn't. Instead he panicked. Suddenly he felt compelled to leave his advertising job and live up to the glittery role of a successful author, lionized by the media and literati on both coasts.

But deep inside he was frightened of the pressure this would bring to his writing and of the professional isolation of being a full-time author. It took Patterson several days to sort out these fears and recognize that he could resolve the panic by a very simple move: Keep his job as creative director at J. Walter Thompson.

Most other people would have jumped at the chance to quit the nine-to-five life, but Jim knew that staying active in both professions was the only way to maintain his professional equilibrium.

HOW TO SURVIVE BURNOUT

The point of this chapter is that if you're not really enjoying your job, perhaps you should be working somewhere else. But what of the person who has loved his job or company, but is getting bored doing the same thing, day after day?

The term for this feeling is burnout. You probably need to make a move, but it may not need to be a permanent career change. There are probably several interim measures you can explore that can function as a step toward a new career or as a rejuvenating break:

• Temporary Reassignment:
Flight attendants are notorious for suffering from burnout, due to long hours, grueling physical demands, and the erratic schedules of their jobs. Some airlines deal with this problem by letting flight attendants move into management, ticketing, or ground service on a trial basis. If they decide they prefer the new position and have done a good job, they may change jobs permanently. If not, they can return to inflight service with some added experience and a new perspective that, ideally, will protect them from future burnout.

• Trade Jobs:
If your company doesn't have such a program, one way around this is to try negotiating with other employees who might be interested in trading jobs with you, and then propose the plan to your supervisor.

• Part-Time Work:
If you have an area of expertise, consider teaching a night class in a local adult education program or writing about the subject for newspapers or magazines. As a doctor or lawyer, you could do some pro bono work in the community to lift yourself above the daily grind. If you've always wanted to write a novel or paint, make that your part-time job.

Theoretically, any of these sideline occupations could blossom into second professions, but in the meantime, they will help you get your mind off your primary job, and use brain skills that currently aren't being tapped.

• Go Back to School:

Most people think of higher education as a ticket to a new career, but it can also serve as a bridge to get you across a burnout phase and into a growth stage in your current profession. Many employers will even foot the tuition bills so you can get the credentials that will make you a more valuable employee. Your courses must relate to the nature of your employer's business, however, though it may be in an area that's new and stimulating to you personally.

• Take a Sabbatical:

My friend Frank Wells spent most of his adult life working his way to the top of the law profession and then the motion picture business, but when he reached his late forties he decided there were other mountains to climb. Literally. It had been his lifelong dream to climb up to the top of the highest mountain on each continent. He finally decided to take a year-long sabbatical as president of Warner Bros. Studios to launch a serious mountaineering expedition. And when he returned to Hollywood, his job was still waiting for him. Today, he's the president of the Walt Disney Company.

KEY POINTS

1. FULFILLED. Our careers and lives are not synonymous. The reality is that your career is simply one of the tools you use to lead a better life.
2. FREE. Find a career you enjoy so much that you'd go to work every day, whether someone paid you for it or not. Be sure the things the career gives you are things that will enhance your life. Your career should *service* your life.
3. HAPPINESS. You will have the most interesting and successful life if you maximize the things you enjoy doing and minimize the things you dislike.
4. QUESTION. Before taking on a new project or client, I always ask myself: "What will this add to my life that I really need or want?" Because, for me, doing the best job for the clients I already have is what's most important. Please use this principle in your career and life as well. It will help you to realize your true goals.

OPTIMISM AND ENTHUSIASM

I am an optimist. It does not seem too much use being anything else.

—WINSTON CHURCHILL

I also take the optimistic view of life. Indeed, what's the point of not believing that anything is possible, that the best is attainable? I always see the glass as half full rather than half empty.

The success of Hands Across America was based on faith. If people didn't believe that others would go out there and hold hands with them across the country, it wouldn't have happened.

> **My job was to create an optimistic perception of its success, because it was necessary for people to believe that they were going to be part of something that was historically significant in order for them to make the commitment.**

Hands Across America is a great example of a project with which we faced every obstacle imaginable and pulled it off, simply by believing in it so strongly. No matter what happened, I knew we would find a way to make it work.

> **Whenever I'm asked to name the one factor that has contributed the most to my personal success, I have to say it's my enthusiasm. Because this enthusiasm is genuine, it's contagious. I can transmit it to those who work with me, and I'm able to use my excitement about a project to successfully attract and excite others. In any business or project, when you're trying to sell something, you constantly have to go up against resistance. Only with a true belief can you work your way through the negatives. I do it, very simply, with enthusiasm and optimism.**

RULE I: HAVE THE RIGHT ATTITUDE

If you let pessimism rule your life, if you refuse to reach for those stars, catch them, and run with them—you haven't got a chance. You can't be successful without deliberately and consciously deciding that you can, in fact, identify your own goals, resolve to realize them, and then set out, step by step, to attain them.

People who have a positive and clear career attitude are the ones who succeed. You can recognize them by the way they do business and by the way they conduct their personal lives. They have a clear, straightforward vision of the world in general and of their goals in particular. They set themselves apart from the crowd behind them because they have identified their goals and present themselves as skilled and talented professionals who are honest without being naive, organized without being rigid, moral without being arrogant, and independent in their thinking without being antagonistic.

Several years ago a young woman answered my ad for a housekeeper. I was surprised to see on her résumé that she held a master's degree in communications. But it didn't take me long to psych out her career strategy. She assumed my furniture was covered with stardust!

A little light housework today, celebrity management tomorrow!

Actually, this was not necessarily a mistake. I believe the foot-in-the-door approach can work if you are talented, ambitious, and willing to prove your worth—if, in other words, you have a positive career attitude.

The lowest mail room position can be a valuable stepping-stone, but only if you excel in that position. You have to make an outstanding impression from the very start, whatever work you do. But the young woman who seemed eager to mop my floor neglected to do just that. Once her foot was inside the door, she barely did what she had been hired to do. She was unenthusiastic, erratic, and showed so little initiative that finally I was forced to fire her.

Some people squander opportunities by looking down their noses at them, others by being too impatient. They expect opportunity to fall neatly in their laps, if not hit them over the head. They find no meaning in any job that isn't the Big Break. The world would be so simple if it worked that way, but it doesn't. Breaks don't just happen. *You have to make your own breaks.* That's why it's so important to have the right attitude about your career.

RULE II: SPREAD THE WORD

I believe in spreading good news. If I'm on the phone with a radio executive and my real objective is to get him to play a record by one of my clients, I will always begin by sharing some bit of good news. Maybe I'll tell him about something wonderful my young daughter did today, or something great that's happened to one of my clients.

In turn, I'll always ask about things that are going on in his or her life, and it's amazing what comes out of that. It engages people and makes them feel involved. Some may be bored with the chat, but most really enjoy sharing good things with you. Down the road, they end up feeling good about your clients and what's happening with them as well.

RULE III: DON'T BE COOL

I've never been very good at pulling off a tough-guy image, and when I began talking publicly about Hands Across America, I realized how pointless it was to even try to be poker-faced.

The media was enthusiastic. Why should I, of all people, try to play it cool? If there was ever a time to be passionate about an idea, this was it. So I began to let people know how strongly I really felt about America's hunger crisis. Immediately, I could feel audiences come alive.

I've applied that same strategy to business dealings, and have gotten the same response. Even when dealing with an arch rival across the table, it's not hard to humanize him or her if you're willing to let your own enthusiasm through.

RULE IV: ALWAYS MIX BUSINESS WITH PLEASURE

Why have a career if nothing about it is fun? You need to enjoy the actual process of your work in order to make your career a success. If nothing in the nitty-gritty of your everyday work appeals to you, then you'd better start looking for another profession.

If, in fact, you're having a good time at work, you're going to be much better at it and considerably more likely to be successful. I want everything I do in business to be fun. I feel that people who are driven by "how much money will I make?" instead of "will I enjoy what I'm doing?" are never satisfied and use up their lives in the pursuit of something of which they can never have enough. But the people who make what they do truly fun and enjoyable, and who are careful to choose the things that fit that mold, are able to make almost every day worthwhile without pursuing some distant, unreachable goal. I know people in business who, if they just made $1 million, they're not happy until they make $2 million; if they have $100 million, they want $200 million. The target keeps moving further away as they keep getting closer.

RULE V: BE REAL

Soon after we had recorded "We Are the World," before we had even given any money out, USA for Africa was honored for its efforts. The awards were given at the University of Southern California. I went down there to represent our organization and pick up our award. I was preceded at the podium by two superb speakers, representing other organizations that were being honored that evening. The first was actress Susan Dey, then appearing on *L.A. Law*, who gave a moving acceptance speech. Then came comedian Harvey Korman, who was of course very funny. As I sat there waiting for my turn, I thought to myself, How can I be anything but anticlimactic in this situation. I turned to USA for Africa's executive director, Marty Rogol, and said, "Help—what do I do?" Marty simply whispered, "Just give them emotion."

I hadn't realized what a very powerful tool any of us have to move an audience. With Marty's advice fresh in my mind, I moved to the podium and allowed my true emotions about the incredible events of the recording session to play out for the audience in front of me. By the end, I was in tears, and the audience was on its feet. I have never forgotten that lesson. There is nothing stronger in any presentation than allowing your emotions, enthusiasm, and passion to carry the day.

A LATE-NIGHT FLIGHT

My favorite story about optimism comes from Dr. Alan Loy McGinnis, the author of a wonderful book, *The Power of Optimism*. He tells of flying home late one night on an airplane during the recession of the early 1980s, when nearly everybody on the flight was cranky except for a salesman in a nearby aisle, who was playing with children and having a great time.

"You're so happy," said Dr. McGinnis. "What do you do?"

"I sell oil-drilling equipment."

At the time, the oil business was one of the industries most hurt by the recession. But, the salesman said, "my company has decided not to participate in the recession. The equipment we build is similar to what our competitors build, but they've cut their services and lowered their prices, and their salesmen are all depressed and unhappy. We've kept our prices the same, and increased our services. If this recession will just last a year or two longer, we can all retire."

So here's an example where somebody took a bad situation and completely turned it around to his advantage, with optimism and enthusiasm.

After reading this story in Dr. McGinnis's book, I told it to my friend Ralph Destino, the chairman of the board of Cartier. Ralph responded the same way I did. He loved the story, and started regularly using it in his daily work.

The recession of the nineties was just beginning, and Ralph went on record in the jewelry industry saying that Cartier had decided "not to participate in the recession." Whenever someone asked how Cartier was reacting to the recession, he would say, "We heard about the recession, we met on the subject, and we decided not to participate this year."

Ralph made a terrific name for himself by being publicly optimistic, and he kept the spirits of his company high at a time when other companies were flagging. "We sell jewelry, watches, leather goods, fragrances, crystal, and porcelain," says Ralph. "So when someone says, 'How's business?' you can always find *some* bright spot. All you have to do is accentuate the positive."

Ralph got a great response from delegates at a 1993 jewelry dealers' convention in New York, where economic forecasters depressed them with gloomy looks into their recessionary crystal ball. Ralph followed them and said he had no forecast to offer, just the facts. "American men and women are not going to stop falling in love, getting engaged, having birthdays, weddings, or children. All of those things are independent of the economy. All of us who make celebration products have all these wonderful occasions in front of us. It's just how you choose to look at the situation."

HOW OPTIMISM HELPED ME OVERCOME A LOSS

One of my immediate goals when I signed Trisha Yearwood was that she would win the coveted Horizon Award at the Country Music Association's annual show. Around award time, Trisha was the odds-on favorite to get it. But in this business nothing is certain, as we soon learned when the award went to Suzy Boggus.

Two things came immediately into my mind. First of all, it was a lot more important for Suzy to win than Trisha, since my client had already won seven major awards that year. Secondly, I thought, Let's focus on what we have, not what we don't have, and that's exactly what I said to Trisha backstage.

Her publicist was in tears, but Trisha took my advice. If you focus on the positives and move ahead, you don't sit there feeling sorry for yourself. You deal with everything in a different way, and come off better to people. Whiners do not win popularity awards.

NO ISN'T IN MY VOCABULARY

At my office, the word "no" simply doesn't exist. If somebody puts up a roadblock, we just have to be more creative in trying to come up with ways to solve the problem.

Take, for instance, my frustrating pursuit to have Kenny Rogers photograph Hillary Rodham Clinton in the White House for our CBS special, *A Day in the Life of Country Music.*

When the Country Music Association asked us to produce the special, we were faced with two important issues: how to create the best show possible, and how to properly service my own clients on a show in a way that would not only satisfy them but would also not make others in the country music field upset with me because I had shown undue favoritism to my own artists.

What I did immediately was look for areas that were natural and fit in with what my clients already do in a typical day on the road. The program was to be shot in one twenty-four-hour day, Friday, May 7, 1993. Twenty-two film crews in twenty-five cities filming forty different country artists at work and play.

On the date we were shooting the show, Travis and Trisha were both booked for a concert in Dallas, so it was obvious that we would cover their performances there. We also set up a Travis visit to a veteran's hospital (he's the honorary chairman for Disabled American Veterans) and for Trisha to promote her Wild Heart perfume with an appearance at a local target store.

Next, we had to come up with something interesting and significant for Kenny Rogers. He's been my client for twenty-seven years and is one of the most successful entertainers in the world.

Kenny's close friend and assistant, Rob Pincus, suggested the idea of Kenny photographing President Clinton, since he had already displayed his presidential camerawork with presidents Carter, Ford, and Reagan in a book of celebrity photos.

My first call was to Clinton press spokeswoman Dee Dee Myers. I had had excellent relations with her during the campaign. She thought it was a good idea and asked me to send her all the information. I shipped off a letter and a copy of Kenny's *Your Friends and Mine* book of photographs.

Then I called producer Harry Thomason (*Evening Shade, Designing Women*) who as everyone knows is an old friend of the Clintons. Harry told me he was on his way to Washington, and that he would take the idea up with the White House while he was there.

Days and weeks went by but nothing happened. Finally, when the shoot date was fast approaching, and when my calls weren't being returned, Kenny suggested calling John Y. Brown, the former governor of Kentucky, another old friend of the Clintons.

By this time, CBS had decided that they would rather have Kenny photograph Mrs. Clinton. Unbeknownst to me, John Y. was somehow able to get to a friend of the First Lady to speak to her about the request.

Suddenly on Wednesday, May 5, at 10 A.M., Mrs. Clinton's appointment secretary called me and said that the First Lady could sit for Kenny Rogers the next day at 3 P.M. I said that the actual *Day in the Life* wasn't until Friday, but was told that Mrs. Clinton would be in Massachusetts on Friday. It was Thursday at 3 P.M. or nothing.

My assistant Laurel Altman, as always, came up with the perfect solution: Have Kenny take the photo on Thursday and then film Kenny, on Friday, May 7, developing the picture in his darkroom at his farm in Georgia.

The point is, we never would have gotten into the White House if I had agreed to take "no" (or the lack of an answer) as final. I knew this was the best way to utilize Kenny Rogers in the show, and I wouldn't let go of it. I didn't have an equally good alternative. I was going to find a way to make this thing happen no matter what. And once we did get into the White House, even the President dropped by to see us and it turned out to be one of the highlights of the special.

Just remember, there isn't anything you can't accomplish if you refuse to take no for an answer.

NO, THE SEQUEL

My friend Dennis Holt, who runs the Western International media-buying service in Los Angeles, has a saying in his office: "Never take no from someone who can't say yes."

Dennis's firm buys advertising for companies, and then places it on radio and television, a once-radical idea that has now become an accepted business practice.

One of his favorite "no" stories concerning a call on a potential client began this way. "The guy told me that he hated my guts, and that he would never do business with me," says Dennis. "He berated me for sixty seconds, which is a long time to take abuse. I ended the phone call by saying, 'I'm putting you down as a firm maybe.'

"I stayed on top of him for ten years, and then I finally got his business. The way I live my life, I never take anything personally. If you have a good product, and believe in yourself, everyone will eventually come around. The way I see it, every media account is mine, but some of them are just being held by somebody else right now."

HOW OPTIMISM CAN GET YOU AHEAD IN BUSINESS

There's a personal manager in Hollywood by the name of Judy Fields. She's a bright, gregarious, funny, confident woman, whom I first met years ago when she was a flight attendant for American Airlines. But even then she was clearly destined for bigger things.

Her first lucky break came when she was a contestant on *Name That Tune*. She broke the show's all-time record by naming all the tunes in eleven seconds. Judy was so engaging and enthusiastic that the producers of the show took a chance and hired her as a contestant coordinator.

So she left the airline industry and spent a couple of years working with contestants in game-show land. I then hired Judy as my assistant. As she moved up, she devoured information about the business and put her own personal career talents to work.

Within two years Judy was a full-time manager, and today Judy has her own company and clients. Within ten years her career went from airlines to TV to personal management, all because she was willing to throw herself enthusiastically into every new challenge that came her way.

Many of the skills that propelled Judy's career forward in entertainment are the same ones she developed working with the airlines. She knew how to charm people and make them feel comfortable. She could make herself attractive without being too alluring or intimidating. She had an incredible sense of humor and was extremely well organized—two qualities absolutely necessary for working under adverse physical conditions.

It didn't matter whether she was pouring coffee at thirty-five thousand feet, soothing a contestant's jangled nerves in the backstage chaos of a TV studio, or discussing a million-dollar contract at my kitchen counter. Judy always got the job done. She remembered everyone's name, even secretaries, which made people all over town feel like they knew her and she knew them. In any business, that access to the "inside track" is an essential career tool.

PESSIMISTS NEED NOT APPLY

Back in the seventies, a former superstar of the sixties came to me for advice. He had recorded more top hits and received more Grammies than anyone else in a brief period of time. He'd even had his own television show. But, for a variety of reasons, his career went into a slump and by the time he came to us for management he'd been losing ground for several years. We didn't think his career was all washed up, but he made it so. Psychologically he refused to accept his decline. In his own mind he was still a star. Instead of developing new material or marketing his act to a new generation, he blamed his problems on everyone but himself. When only a few fans showed up for a performance, he would walk out on them. He turned on colleagues and supporters who worked for him and burned bridges on every front. It was as though he wanted personally to destroy what little career he still had. Instead of admitting that he had lost his drawing power, he blamed the hotel or the club for not promoting his show. He still expected to be treated as a superstar when in fact his star had long set. The good news is that eventually he was able to break out of the emotional downhill cycle and make a comeback. He then restored his public image and regained some of his popularity.

THE ENTHUSIASTIC GAMBLER

How did someone who had never produced a TV movie sell a network a Movie of the Week starring a man who had never acted in his life? With enthusiasm.

After looking at the cover of Kenny Rogers's *Gambler* album, with Kenny decked out in period western garb, I became convinced that the look of the album and the popularity of the song would translate into a terrific TV film.

Backstage at an awards show, I walked up to CBS execs Bernie Sofronski and Fred Rappaport, and pulled out a poster of Kenny as the gambler. "Wouldn't it be wonderful to do a movie with Kenny playing this character?" I asked. Their response: "Sold."

I genuinely believed that a very successful TV movie could be created around Kenny Rogers and *The Gambler*. It didn't matter that neither Kenny nor I had any experience. My enthusiasm for the project made it happen. Clearly we were onto something. Years later, as I write this, we are beginning production on *Gambler V*.

OPTIMISM AND LOSS, PART II

When my mother Billie died in 1988 at age seventy-six, people said to me, "What a tragedy. She was such a wonderful woman."

I agreed with them. Mom was absolutely wonderful, but I didn't see the fairly quick death of a seventy-six-year-old woman, who had had such a wonderful life and who in the last few years of her life had seen her children and grandchildren achieve great success, as a tragedy.

My mother had a stroke on Easter Sunday, but remained alive for two more weeks. During those two weeks, she was able to hear from all of us about how much we loved her. We had been told by the doctor on the day she died that she would be an invalid. I don't believe she heard the comment, but somewhere inside of her she just decided to check out because she didn't want to be a burden on anybody.

A tragedy is when an eight-year-old child is killed by a stray bullet. When a seventy-six-year-old woman dies, and does so in a way that's not overly painful, I don't view that as a tragedy. It is a sad but unchangeable part of human existence. I know that's the way my mom (a steadfast optimist) would have viewed it as well.

HARRY CHAPIN AND OPTIMISM

I was with singer Harry Chapin at the Forum in 1980, watching the Los Angeles Lakers on the night Ronald Reagan swept into office with all those new conservative senators. At half time we went in to the press lounge to see the results of the election on TV. One by one, each of the candidates Harry had worked so hard to support were being defeated by the Moral Majority and the Reagan landslide.

But instead of getting depressed, Harry simply said, "Ken, I'm sorry, but I have to get on a plane and get back East to go to Washington as soon as possible. The Republicans got elected on a law-and-order platform, and this is a terrific opportunity. I want to go back so I can show them how reducing the amount of hunger, poverty, and homelessness can have enormous impact on law and order in our cities."

And with that, he left. He didn't even stay for the second half of the game. That's an optimist!

KEY POINTS

1. FERVOR. Enthusiasm is the one factor that has contributed the most to my personal success. In any business or project where you're trying to sell something, you constantly have to go up against resistance. Only with true belief can you work your way through the negatives. I do it with enthusiasm and optimism.

2. WASTE. Some people squander opportunities by looking down at them. They expect opportunity to fall neatly in their laps. But breaks don't *just* happen. You have to make your own breaks. That's why it's so important to have the right attitude about your career.

3. GLOWING. I believe in letting your enthusiasm and passion for a project come shining through. It's pointless to try to be poker-faced with an arch rival across the table. It's not hard at all to humanize him with zing.

4. YES. There isn't anything you can't accomplish if you refuse to take "no" for an answer. At my office, the word "no" doesn't exist. If there's a roadblock, we just have to be more creative in trying to come up with ways to solve the problem.

5. UPBEAT. Look for positive opportunities in everything that happens—even the most negative career events.

STRATEGY VI
LIFE IS A CONTACT SPORT

Be nice to people on your way
up because you'll meet them
on your way down.

—WILSON MIZNER

I truly believe that life is a contact sport. You never know just who you'll meet and what role they might later play in your career or your life.

It was an electrician, for instance, who plugged Travis Tritt into a career in the music business. And it was singing demos with the then unknown Garth Brooks that led to Trisha Yearwood's career success.

A wide-ranging network of friends and business acquaintances can benefit anyone's career. What some people just starting out don't realize is that everyone has some kind of network. It begins in childhood and develops gradually over the years. Your first resources are likely to be personal friends, family members, college acquaintances, and former teachers. Later contacts emerge through coworkers, bosses, business mentors, and even the young people who come to you for advice in building their careers. All these contacts are potentially useful to you, so keep track of them.

> In a way, contacts are like the building blocks of a career. You start with relatively few and keep adding and multiplying until you have a strong, interlocking web of people whose talents and reputations help boost your career.

In the age of computers, it's simple to keep your entire network up to date. Create a mailing list of everyone you deal with on a permanent file and use it frequently. Send out announcements, Christmas cards, informal notes about what's happening with you.

Networking is certainly one of the buzzwords in today's society. Rightfully so. Networking is one of the least expensive, easiest-to-use tools to assist you in building your career. It is important to network, both with and without a purpose. By this, I mean there are times when you want to comb your network of friends and acquaintances with a specific objective in mind, such as finding a lead on a new job. But even more frequently, you will want to network, simply to build the range and scope of your contacts for future opportunities.

NETWORKING

Shirley Hufstedler, the former U.S. secretary of education, decided to become a lawyer at a time—hard as it may seem to believe—when most major law schools refused to admit women. But Hufstedler refused to take "no" for an answer. She found one school that would take her—Stanford University—and became one of just five women to enter its law program in 1946.

Networking became her key to success.

She joined the *Law Review*, where she made a number of valuable contacts among her peers. But after graduating, Hufstedler had to get over another hurdle. She was faced with the field's notorious discrimination against women. But she didn't let that stop her. Undaunted, she called all the Stanford law graduates practicing in Los Angeles to ask about possible openings. One of them hired her to do some work for him. From there she gradually edged her way into general practice.

YOU NEVER KNOW JUST WHO YOU'LL MEET

Let me tell you about how an accidental meeting—someone I came into contact with for maybe thirty minutes—paid off six months later with a job for his daughter.

I had once attempted to buy the screen rights to a story about a man who had organized a football team at a detention camp for teenage multiple offenders. Through this process, he had helped to straighten out many of the kids.

The deal never went through, but six months later the coach called to say that his daughter was looking for a summer job in public relations: Did I know of any openings?

So I picked up the phone and called Kenny Rogers's publicist, Cheryl Kagan, at the large firm of Rogers & Cowan. Cheryl told me that R&C hired interns, and that she would be happy to interview the coach's daughter. She got the job, and at the end of the summer, they offered her a full-time position.

The moral: I was someone her father hardly knew, but I still made a call for his daughter and I happened to be able to open the door. It never hurts to ask, because the worst that could happen is that someone might just say "no."

Almost all of us have some contacts, be it through a distant relative, an acquaintance, a teacher in school, a coworker, or some other person. Ask all your friends and family about any contacts, no matter how remote, in the field or endeavor you've chosen. Use them!

TREAT EVERYONE AS IMPORTANT TO YOU: SOMEDAY THEY REALLY MAY BE

When I was coproducing *The Smothers Brothers Comedy Hour* in the sixties, the cue card boy was a kid named Jeff Margolis. We became friends, and today he is one of the top TV directors in Hollywood. You see his name on the credits every year for the Oscars, and many other shows. Had I dismissed him back then as "just the cue card boy," we might not have stayed in touch. As it is, we have remained friendly and still occasionally work together. No matter what field you're in, you'll be amazed at how many of the people you know and work with now will end up in key positions that are important to you sometime in the future. The world truly is a small place.

BARTER

One of the best ways of getting your foot in the door, is to barter your skills and contacts. You can trade your expertise on the computer, guitar, or whatever. If it costs you $1,000 to make a demo at the recording studio, perhaps instead you can get the fee down by offering to teach guitar lessons, paint the walls, type up fliers, or do something else that would be of service to the potential contact—the owner of the studio.

You can use these skills as an entrée point.

Get really good at something, because in today's specialized marketplace, anything you're reasonably good at is something you can barter with.

CHANCE MEETINGS

During my UCLA astronomy course, I met a fellow student named Ann Drechtrah. At the coffee break, I learned that she had produced a number of the PBS *Cosmos* episodes. I ended up bringing her in to work on a project for me. Then she got me involved with one of her projects. All from a chance meeting at a class.

One of my most successful chance meetings happened at the 1992 Grammys, where I ran into Jay Coleman, who specializes in putting corporate America together with music personalities. I told him how I'd been working with this great, young, attractive country singer named Trisha Yearwood, and he mentioned that Revlon was looking for a female country personality for its new campaign. A few weeks later, we were signing papers to have Trisha front Revlon's multimillion-dollar campaign for a new fragrance called Wild Heart.

HOW I PLAYED BASKETBALL WITH THE FUTURE PRESIDENT AND ENDED UP WITH TWO GREAT SEATS FOR THE INAUGURATION

In the summer of 1991, when I was managing Burt Reynolds's career, a student from the town of Evening Shade, Arkansas (yes, there really is a such a place), wrote to Burt. She said she went to Evening Shade High School, and asked him to give the commencement speech for the twenty-five graduating seniors. "Everybody at school told me you would never come," she wrote. "But my parents said I had nothing to lose, so I might as well try."

Burt was taken by the letter and decided to go. So I scheduled one of Burt's one-man shows in Little Rock the day after the commencement to make a weekend of it. Hillary Clinton, then the governor's wife, decided to come along with us.

We flew to the town of Evening Shade on a very small plane. For two hours up there and two hours back I was literally sitting knee to knee with Hillary and we talked the whole time.

Back in Little Rock, I checked into my hotel and was about to go to sleep around midnight, when the phone rang. "Ken, this is Bill Clinton. My wife says you like to play basketball. Would you like to play tomorrow?" After I said yes, the then-governor said, "I'll go check out the Y and call you in the morning."

Promptly at 8 A.M. the next morning, Clinton called to say he was at the Y and that we should meet at 9 A.M. to begin the game.

When I got to the Y, there were about five to six guys warming up in this rickety downtown Little Rock gym. Clinton was still in the weight room working out, but when he showed up on the court, nobody made any particular fuss about him, even though he was the governor of the state.

We played for two hours and then I went back to the hotel. That night, Bill and Hillary came backstage at Burt's show. Bill asked how long I would be in town, and I told him I'd be leaving the next morning at 6:30. "I'll send my car to take you to the airport," he said. "Don't bother," I said, but he insisted.

The next morning, up drives this car, with Bill Clinton himself at the wheel. He's in shorts and with cup of coffee in hand. He leaps out, grabs my bags, drives me around town, and then takes me to the airport, where he carries my bags in and checks me in at the counter. At that point I offered to buy him breakfast. I felt I better do something.

Burt had told me the night before that Clinton was going to run for president, but he hadn't announced his plans yet. I assumed Clinton would be hitting me up for a contribution and or support. There always seems to be some ulterior motive with politicians. Alan Cranston, the former California senator, took my wife and me to dinner one night, and we sat there the whole night, wondering, Why is Alan Cranston taking us to dinner? Finally, during dessert, he looked at me, and said, "Is your friend Peter Ueberroth going to run against me this year?"

But at breakfast, Bill never asked for a thing. He told me that nobody could beat George Bush in 1992, but that he was thinking of running anyway, to try to make a credible showing and come back again in 1996. He called it a case of being realistic and optimistic at the same time. But never once did he ask for my help.

In fact, he was so low key that five months later I had to call to volunteer my services. I had to get on the phone and say, "Hey, I'm a resource. Use me."

I ended up being active in the campaign, consulting on media issues, and went on to coproduce, with Quincy Jones, the event at the Lincoln Memorial that kicked off the Inaugural activities with a restaging of dozens of superstars singing "We Are the World." As a result, my family and I had wonderful seats at the actual Inauguration a few days later.

The moral to the story is that you never know who you're going to meet or how they can help you later on down the road. Life really is a contact sport.

My first impression of Bill Clinton was so favorable that I was anxious to join his campaign. (It didn't hurt that I also agreed with his politics.) And it certainly doesn't hurt me to now have a friend in the White House.

CONTACT SPORTS REALLY DO PAY OFF

OK, so not everyone gets to play basketball with the future pres., but whether you're into sports or not, if you want to get ahead in whatever business you're in, you should really pursue all company sports activities with an eye toward career advancement.

Remember on the old episodes of *The Honeymooners*, how Ralph Kramden always wanted to play golf or pool with the boss, even though he didn't know anything about the sport? "This is how you get places," Ralph told pal Ed Norton, "socializing with the higher-ups."

What was true in the 1950s remains the same in the 1990s: Everyone's equal on the playing field, and there's no better way to get the attention of upper management than by playing games with them.

Sun Microsystems has company hockey games; at General Chemical Group the sport is power-walking at lunchtime. At computer giant Microsoft, employees with common interests (car rallies, sailing, rock climbing, flag football, paragliding) form groups and send out information and schedules over E-mail.

Robert Teufel, the president of Rodale Press, has been known to sweat with employees in a morning exercise class several days a week at the company's headquarters in Emmaus, Pennsylvania. "Those people who choose to participate get a chance to communicate with him differently," Budd Coates, director of Rodale's gym, told *Business Week*.

One of the hottest tickets in Hollywood used to be former NBC chief Brandon Tartikoff's weekly Saturday baseball game. It was simply one of the best networking opportunities in town, with a team full of network execs, producers, actors, and writers. Brandon had a three-year waiting list of new players who were dying to get on the team because of the unbelievable contact sport possibilities.

But while I do recommend being a part of the sports team with your colleagues, think hard about exactly how badly you want to win the game. Microsoft's Jon Staenberg told *Business Week* that after he slaughtered a higher-up in racquetball, the manager's attitude toward him completely changed. "Politically, I probably shouldn't have beaten him," he said.

BRIDGES

Business negotiations, if handled shrewdly, can beef up your career network. Negotiations viewed as ruthless, one-shot propositions—milk the other side for as much as possible and make your get-away—may benefit your employer or client, but they're liable to damage your personal career in the long run by alienating the people with whom you're negotiating.

As a rule, I approach each deal not as a single transaction, but as a starting point for a long-term relationship. Several years ago, for instance, we negotiated an agreement for Kenny Rogers to do some promotional work for Chrysler. We knowingly took less money than we might have demanded and used the initial partnership to get to know Joe Campana and John Damoose of Chrysler's marketing team, and to find out what Chrysler's problems and needs were. From this vantage point we went on to work together on subsequent ventures.

Successful networking presumes good relations with people you meet throughout your life. If there's one hard-and-fast rule it's this: DON'T BURN BRIDGES! Yesterday's foe may be tomorrow's friend.

Back in the 1960s I managed a group called the Pair Extraordinaire, and they were signed to ABC Records. The president of the label flat out reneged on part of our deal, and gave us such poor treatment that I swore to him on the phone that I would never do business with him again.

I lost my head, something I wouldn't recommend others doing.

As it turned out, fifteen years later, he became the president of Motown, and shortly thereafter I began managing Lionel Richie. Luckily for both of us, he had forgotten about our run-in years earlier. And fortunately for me, I was in the driver's seat, because Lionel was currently Motown's most successful act.

We had both learned by then, and our relationship was much more successful the second time around.

THE ELECTRICIAN AND THE SINGER

One of my favorite stories showing how the most unlikely person can end up being your best overall contact concerns my client Travis Tritt. (For the complete story, read the chapter on Careers.)

Travis was knocking around Atlanta, trying to find a way to get into the music business. He was playing every small club, the kinds of places, Travis likes to say, where when you went in they gave you a knife and a gun at the door so everybody would be equal inside.

Travis noticed that the Marlboro Talent Search was coming through town, and decided to enter the competition. The only problem was that he needed a demo tape, and he didn't have enough money to get one made.

An electrician friend of Travis told him that he was in the process of installing a small studio at the home of a Warner Bros. executive, and said he would ask if Travis could use the studio to cut a tape.

Danny Davenport, the exec, agreed, and when he heard Travis sing, he turned to him and said, "Where have you been hiding?"

It took awhile, but Danny eventually got Travis a deal at Warner Bros., and today Travis is one of the label's biggest-selling acts.

All thanks to his friendship with an electrician that on paper really wouldn't have suggested Travis's first major show-business break.

HOW I GOT INTO SHOW BUSINESS
THANKS TO CONTACTS

I'm the son of a prominent University of California law professor and grew up in Berkeley and Los Angeles. I can't sing, dance, or play an instrument, but I've always loved music. When I was in high school, I planned on becoming a microbiologist, but fairly early in the game it dawned on me that I didn't have enough of the personal traits that are important for success in that occupation. Most of my skills were more social and outgoing, and I was very weak at math. Using my creative talents, I decided to go into advertising, although while in school my hobby was producing concerts on the side. Had it not been for Lou Gotlieb, I probably would have continued my studies in engineering at the University of California-Berkeley, and not gone into management. But Lou changed all of that.

Back in 1956, when I was eighteen and new to college, I produced my first concert at UC Berkeley. It was a general admission, 75-cent show featuring a group called the Gateway Singers.

I worked extremely hard to promote the show, but since we didn't have any advance sales, there was no way of knowing whether the show would be a smash or a flop.

Back before I knew about the powers of optimism, I was so nervous about the outcome that I convinced myself no one would show up, and that the concert would be a big bust. Luckily, I was very wrong. Instead there was a long line of people circling Wheeler Auditorium waiting to get in, and the Gateway Singers were very impressed.

The Gateway Singers eventually broke up, but I kept in contact with Lou, who formed a new group, the Limeliters. I booked them for several concerts at UC as well.

After graduating from UC, I moved from Berkeley to Boston, where I attended the Harvard Business School. But whenever I came home to see my parents, I would often visit the hungry i folk club in

San Francisco, the center for topical comedy (Mort Sahl, Dick Gregory) and the popular folk trios of the day, like the Kingston Trio; Peter, Paul and Mary; and the Limeliters.

I remained friendly with the Limeliters—Lou Gotlieb, Glenn Yarborough, and Alex Hassilev. Lou, who has a Ph.D. in psychology, was and is a very funny man. With his wonderful sense of humor, he would play off Glenn, who had the voice of an angel, and Alex, the handsome sex symbol of the group.

I loved these guys because they were the intellectual and humorous bridge between the sometimes esoteric approach of pure folk music and the performance values of popular entertainment.

The day before I was ready to return to Harvard from my Christmas vacation, Lou called. "We've been talking," he said, "and we'd decided that we'd like you to come work for us as our executive secretary."

My response was perhaps the gutsiest thing I've ever done in my life, if you consider my age and inexperience. "I didn't go to the Harvard Business School to be anyone's executive secretary," I said. "If you guys decide that you ever need a manager, call me." Lou thanked me for my candor and hung up.

A few days later, when I arrived back in Cambridge, there was this long, funny rambling letter from Lou waiting for me. He asked me to be their manager. I called Lou and said that's great, but that the group would have to wait until I graduated in May.

At the time, the Limelighters weren't that well known outside of San Francisco, so it wasn't like I was taking a job with an established pop group. This was totally speculative. In fact, I turned down job offers from Time Inc., Procter & Gamble, and the J. Walter Thompson advertising agency to do it. Why? As a high school concert promoter, I had obviously been stung by the lure of show business, but I was also attracted by the idea of working for myself. I saw management as a way to have the freedom of running a small business.

I actually began working for the Limeliters before I graduated. I went to Chicago during the Easter school break. The group was playing at a popular Chicago nightclub called Mr. Kelley's. It was in the Windy City that I got the surprise of my life. I went to their hotel, and as I opened the door to Lou's room, I heard Alex say, "That's it. We're breaking up."

I immediately flashed upon what a poor career decision I had made. But what I didn't realize was that the Limeliters would break up practically every day. Their charm on stage was that they were three distinct and different personalities, but offstage, their experience, attitudes, and lifestyles were so different that they couldn't agree on anything.

In fact, the reason each of them had liked the idea of hiring a young kid with no experience to be their manager was because they figured that since I was so green, they could control the other two through me.

It was quite an instant education in management psychology. I had endless separate meetings with each of them. Each member would buttonhole me to sell me on their point of view, and tell me why the others were wrong.

I would listen to all three, each distinctly different from the other, and learn something from each one. Then, when we had a general meeting, they would disagree and I would make the decision.

The main thing I learned from the experience was that I wasn't afraid to try anything. By turning down the job offer at first, all I did was whet their appetite for me, and I found out that I wasn't such a bad negotiator after all.

Again, you never know just who you'll meet and what role they will have in your career. Had I not produced that concert for the Gateway Singers, had it not gone well, had Lou Gottlieb not been impressed with the work—who knows what might have happened? The idea of a career as a personal manager was something I had never thought of, or even realized existed. It was just thrust onto me when the Limelighters offered me a job.

The day after the Limeliters broke up, I signed another Bay Area folk combo—the Smothers brothers. By the mid-seventies, I was not only managing the Smothers, I was also coproducing their CBS variety series *The Smothers Brothers Comedy Hour*. I also managed their stable of repertory players—Pat Paulsen, Bob Einstein (he's now known as Showtime's "Super Dave"), John Hartford, and Mason (Classical Gas) Williams, along with a rock group that had made several appearances on the Smothers program—The First Edition. Best known at the time for their hits, "Ruby, Don't Take Your Love to Town," and "I Just Dropped In to See What My Condition Was In,"

The First Edition featured a bass player I was particularly fond of. His name: Kenny Rogers.

A lot of other managers have used the field as a stepping-stone to other avenues of the business, (Mace Neufeld in movies, Bernie Brillstein in television, Irving Azoff as the president of MCA and Giant Records,) but I have never let it go: It is something I know I am good at, and still enjoy tremendously. More important, to walk away from management would cut off the source of most of the opportunities I have had to do other challenging and exciting things in the entertainment business. Almost everything I have accomplished has come as a direct or indirect result of my work as a personal manager.

However, I once did almost get out of the business. In 1969, a few months before CBS canceled *The Smothers Brothers Comedy Hour*, I had a falling out with the Smothers brothers. Fortunately, I was able to work out a decent settlement with them.

I figured I had enough to live in the Caribbean for a dozen years, so my then-wife Jinx and I headed south, where we rented a sailboat and got completely away from the rat race. A month later, my attorney, Frank Wells (now the president of The Walt Disney Company), wired me on the island of Barbados and told me that the deal had fallen apart. He suggested strongly that we come back immediately.

When I returned, all of my other clients—Bob Einstein, John Hartford, Pat Paulsen, Mason Williams, Jennifer Warnes, Kenny Rogers, and The First Edition urged me to get back in the management business.

This was a very rough period for me, but I realized that these people really needed my help. Personal management was something I seemed to be good at, and I enjoyed being needed, so I agreed to continue. And I've never regretted that decision.

KEY POINTS

1. COMMUNICATION. Life truly is a contact sport. You never know just who you'll meet and what role that person might later play in your life or career.
2. NETWORKING. Contacts are the building blocks of a career. You begin with few and keep adding and multiplying until you have a strong, interlocking web of people whose talents and reputation help boost your career.
3. CHANNELS. Everyone has some kind of network. It begins in childhood and develops gradually over the years. Your first resources will be friends and family, but they will continually expand, and if you think really hard, you'll realize that your immediate contact base is actually a lot wider than first imagined. Build on it.
4. CYBER-CONTACTS. In the computer age, it's simple to keep your network up to date. Create a mailing list of everyone you deal with on a permanent file and use it frequently.
5. COOL. Don't burn bridges. Yesterday's foe may be tomorrow's friend.

EVERYTHING IN LIFE IS AN OPPORTUNITY

*Opportunities are usually
disguised as hard work, so most
people don't recognize them.*

—ANN LANDERS

In 1975, I lost virtually everything I had. I had sunk all of my money into producing *The Doo-Dah Gang*, a live production show featuring a group of 1920s-style singers and dancers at the Flamingo Hilton in Las Vegas. When the show didn't catch on, I took a real beating—to the tune of $150,000.

But *The Doo-Dah Gang* wasn't my only problem. The First Edition, my main source of income at the time, suddenly broke up, I was thirty-five years old and had been working for myself all of my adult life, but had to make a major life adjustment by going to work for manager Jerry Weintraub. In the seventies, Jerry was the most successful personal manager in the entertainment business. His clients included John Denver, the Carpenters, Bob Dylan, and Neil Diamond.

For the first time, I had to answer to somebody. Some could have viewed this as a real let-down and negative, but I saw the situation as a major opportunity. Despite the fact that it wasn't the ideal working atmosphere for me, it thrust me back into the center of the entertainment community. I established contacts that I never could have made on my own. At any one time you might run into the likes of Bob

Dylan, Jimmy Carter, or Col. Tom Parker in the hallways of Jerry's company. Instead of a setback, this situation actually was the beginning of the incredible run of success I've enjoyed ever since.

I look at almost everything that happens in my life as an opportunity. In your career and life as well, even the negatives can become an opportunity for advancement and success.

A few years ago, for instance, I was managing singer Olivia Newton-John, who told me that she wanted to have a baby, and she wanted also to fulfill her life's dream by recording an album of lullabies.

My career proposal: Go ahead, get pregnant, and get the album recorded. Then, a year from now, you can go on TV talk shows with the new album, and talk about how you put your baby to sleep with the record.

"Ken Kragen," she said to me. "You're the only person who can make having a baby into a career event."

As for Kenny Rogers, I helped him turn his love of photography into a career opportunity. I had noticed how Kenny was really producing some outstanding camera work and thoroughly enjoying doing it, so I encouraged him to publish it in book form. We sold two books of Kenny's photography to publishers, arranged several major exhibitions, and even fashioned a TV special, *Kenny Rogers' America*, around his hobby. The special was Kenny's look at America and the people of the country. Then we arranged to have him go on the *Oprah Winfrey Show*, where Kenny photographed Oprah on the air to promote both his TV special and his book.

Since then, we have often used Kenny's hobbies—be they photography, golf, or tennis—as career tools. We take something Kenny has fun doing and use it as an opportunity to take his career into a different arena.

THE CASE OF THE STOLEN STATUE

Put yourself into the shoes of a McDonald's exec. A giant Ronald McDonald statue has been stolen from one of your Pittsburgh properties, and you receive a ransom note demanding forty million Big Macs and Cokes. How do you respond?

Well, first you put your security team on it, and they work with the police. Together they find the perpetrators: two college kids, who stole the statue as a fraternity prank.

So now what do you do? Do you prosecute them to the fullest extent of the law, as a deterrent to other would-be McDonald's vandalizers? The down side is the public relations nightmare of Big Ol' McDonald's picking on these two, poor college kids. The alternative is not to prosecute at all, and laugh the situation off, but is that going to encourage others to break the law without punishment?

This was the negative situation my friend Dick Starmann, a McDonald's senior vice president, found himself in a few years ago. "Because of the seriousness of the situation, we got into a great internal debate in the company about how to handle this," says Dick. "These were young people involved, and no one was hurt. We as a company didn't want to ruin the lives of these young people. But on the other side of the coin, if we didn't prosecute, others might do exactly what these kids did."

Dick turned a potentially negative situation into a positive opportunity when he came up with a brilliant compromise solution: he had the company lawyers approach the judge to recommend an alternative to jail time. The kids could instead serve as weekend volunteers for two months at the Ronald McDonald House, a home for kids with cancer.

"They returned the statue," says Dick, "and at the end of two months, it was stricken from their records. This went from being a very negative situation into a total positive, where we turned lemon into a lemonade. Everybody won, even the young people, who really enjoyed volunteering." And learned a lot from it.

The potential for negative publicity was turned into a positive for McDonald's. It solved the problem and focused attention instead on the Ronald McDonald House, showing how the Golden Arches give back to the community.

THE VISA CARD

Here's a fun example of how to turn a potential negative into a real opportunity. It comes courtesy of another friend, Jim Morey, who like me is also a personal manager. A few years ago Jim decided to teach his children the true meaning of charity at Christmas time. He told his three children—two girls and a boy—that they would receive just one gift that year, explaining that the additional money they would have spent would instead be used to buy gifts for the underprivileged children.

The daughters asked for dolls; the son, Jason, refused to commit. Finally, at the dinner table a week before Christmas, Jim said, "Jason, come on, what do you want?"

"I've finally decided," said Jason. "Dad, I want my own Visa card."

Here was a five-year-old boy, faced with getting only one Christmas gift, and he viewed it not as a potential problem, but in fact a terrific opportunity.

THE MODEL, THE ACCIDENT, AND THE STARRY EYES

Cheryl Shuman was just on the verge of beginning a promising modeling career in 1983 when her car skidded on an icy road and she hit another car head-on. She went through the windshield, and ended up with a fractured leg and shattered face.

Her days as a model were over. But Cheryl didn't view that life change negatively. "I think it was probably one of the best things that ever happened to me," she told *Forbes*.

Cheryl moved from Cleveland to sunny California, to start over in a warmer climate, where she got a job selling eyeglasses at a trendy optical shop. On the surface, this would appear to be a dead-end job, but Cheryl turned it into an opportunity.

After a studio propmaster came in one day hunting for glasses for Shirley MacLaine to wear in the TV mini-series *Out on a Limb*, Cheryl had a brainstorm: Why not take lots of different eyeglass styles to the set so the stars could try them on?

She quit her job and started her own business, taking cash advances on her credit cards, and getting eyeglass manufacturers to give her ninety-day terms. Within two months, she had sold $14,000 worth of eyeglasses.

Her Starry Eyes Optical Services grossed $20 million in 1992, selling eye wear for TV and the movies and to stars like Mel Gibson and Demi Moore, who prefer housecalls to going out in public to shop. When you view everything in life as happening for a good reason, it's amazing how often it works out that way.

THE OPPORTUNITY OF SPEAKING UP

During my stint with the Smothers brothers, we hired a management consultant to look at our operation and show us where we needed to make some changes. Ironically, one of the first suggestions he made was for me to start making Tom and Dick more aware of the work I was doing for them. He pointed out that not only were my contributions being discounted, but the Smothers brothers needed to know exactly how I was managing their career. He said Tom and Dick were only seeing the tip of the iceberg.

So I began to write them memos about my decisions, and in fact became known as the "mad memo writer." The result was an amazing opportunity: I started receiving more credit, and the brothers participated more actively in directing their own career.

When you've made a significant contribution at work you deserve credit, period. You don't have to be obnoxious about it, but make sure that you receive your due recognition, be it a special award, mention in the company newsletter, a promotion, a raise, or simply a vote of thanks from your boss.

THE LOST VOICE

Here's someone else who took a potential negative disaster and turned it into an overwhelming life-changing positive.

Philip Payne's career goal: to be a missionary spreading the gospel of the Evangelical Free Church around the globe. But then, in Japan during the early 1980s, he suddenly lost his voice and his life's work came to a crashing halt.

He returned to the United States in 1983 for voice therapy and resumed biblical research and writing. He also started using computers for his studies, and began investigating a way for the Apple Macintosh computer font system to type in Japanese, Greek, and Hebrew.

A computer specialist taught him how to create fonts for those languages, and Philip took it from there. A few months later, a Macintosh-user magazine did a story on his font program, and then unsolicited orders began pouring in. Four months after his first lesson, he had made his first mail-order sale. Within a year, he had a new career and programs supporting 160 different languages.

His programs are so popular now that even the White House uses them for Russian documents. When Secretary of State George Schultz left office, he presented to his Soviet counterpart, Eduard Shevardnadze, a bilingual Russian and English version of Carl Sandburg's congressional address on Abraham Lincoln, printed with Philip Payne's font program.

ORGANIZATION AND DELEGATION

I'll never forget what the dean told me on my first day at Harvard Business School: "From this day forward, you will always have more work than is humanly possible to do. Those of you who are successful will determine what to do and what not to do."

He was absolutely right. Prioritizing what I will do for my clients and what they will do for themselves is one of my most important functions as a personal manager. It is also crucial for anyone's professional survival.

The person who knows how to organize creates an enormous opportunity for him or herself because the end result is a more efficient operation and more free time.

Take a hard look at yourself and your professional ambitions, and then target the goals that are critical to your advancement. Save for yourself the goals that you alone can accomplish. Then delegate the jobs that can be performed best by someone else. That will ensure that you have time to do what you excel at.

I have found that strong, dedicated people who are workaholics are often overly possessive about their work. I must confess, however, that I am not personally great at delegating. I used to feel that only if I did something myself would it get done the way I thought it should be. But over the years, I've learned not to get bogged down in details, and so I've surrounded myself with people who are great at their jobs. This has given me the confidence to trust others to take on some of the tasks I simply don't have the time to do.

LOST BUSINESS

Whenever a client has left me, my first reaction isn't, "What am I going to do?" but instead, "Boy, I'm sure glad I won't have to deal with those problems anymore," or "Isn't it great to have more time to spend with my family?" or "I wonder what's out there that I could take on and do next?"

I have this undying belief that the future will work itself out. That whatever comes next will be even better and more exciting. I have enough confidence in my own abilities to be secure about the future.

Take, for example, the time two of my former managers, Harriet Sternberg and Gary Borman, left to set up their own company. They took with them five artists (including the Bee Gees) and three employees. On paper, that looked like a potential disaster. But it wasn't.

I sat down after they left and took a close look at the situation. Even though Harriet and Gary were excellent managers, and some of the artists that went with them had terrific economic potential, I was still saving more than $300,000 in salaries and expenses that year. More important, their departure left me almost completely free of the kind of administrative role which is neither one of my strengths nor something I enjoy.

I no longer had to worry about how Gary or Harriet's careers were doing, or deal with the many questions that arose every day concerning their clients, on which they often came to me for advice. So while I had obviously lost some income, and my company had shrunk in size, I viewed it not as a negative, but as a terrific *opportunity*, to get back to doing full time what I enjoyed most: managing my own clients and producing their projects and TV shows.

KEY POINTS

1. FORTUNE. Everything that happens in life is an opportunity. In your life and career, even the negatives can become an opportunity for advancement and success.
2. RESULT. If you believe that everything in life happens for a good reason, somehow things really seem to work out that way.
3. ORDER. The person who knows how to organize creates an enormous opportunity for him or herself because the end result is a more efficient operation and more free time.
4. ATTITUDE. Even the loss of business gains you something: free time or the ability to pursue new challenges.

ABSOLUTE HONESTY IS THE BEST GIMMICK

*Always do right. It will gratify
some and astonish the rest.*

—MARK TWAIN

Back in the 1700s, Frederick the Great, the king of Prussia, arranged an inspection tour of the Berlin prison. Prisoners fell on their knees before him, all vigorously protesting their innocence. But one man alone remained silent and aloof.

"You there, why are you here?" Frederick called to him.

"Armed robbery, Your Majesty."

"And you are guilty?"

"Yes indeed, Your Majesty. I entirely deserve my punishment."

Frederick summoned the warden. "Release this guilty wretch at once," he said. "I will not have him kept in this prison where he will corrupt all the fine, innocent people who occupy it!"

Honesty can truly disarm. It's an extremely easy way to stand out and be unique.

> **I believe that you can get business to beat a path to your door by being the most honest person around. I've built an entire career on it, and think you can too.**

Frankly, I can't tell you of a more satisfying or effective tool for your career than honesty. Total, absolute honesty. Honesty in everything, in every dealing.

For example, Kenny Rogers calls me and says, "Please ask [CBS Entertainment president] Jeff Sagansky about something," and let's say I forget to do it. What do I say to Kenny when he calls for an answer? That I called Sagansky several times, but he never called me back? No, I say, "Kenny, I forgot. I'm sorry, but I forgot." Otherwise, when he runs into Jeff and says, "Why don't you return my manager's calls?" I'm caught in a lie. Equally important, I have strengthened my credibility with Kenny by being honest and telling him something that is not apparently in my best interests.

A person needs only to catch you in one lie or fabrication to lose confidence and trust in you forever. Kenny and I both used to work with someone who was a chronic white-liar. None of the lies that he told were major, but he seemed unable to tell the straight truth about anything! As a result, we rarely trusted anything that he said, and he had far less significance in our lives than if we were not constantly faced with this unfortunate habit.

I once had a very difficult negotiation with a group of lawyers and principals who were demanding a large sum of money they felt I owed them on a production we had done together. We all sat down and I began with absolute honesty to lay out the facts of the situation. Fortunately, I have a reputation for telling the truth at all times, so what I was saying held credibility.

But I was also honest about the negative and positive sides of what I had done. By the end of the meeting the two principals were arguing with their own lawyers that they, not I, should absorb the losses and that they should go to bat with the third parties involved to see that I was fairly compensated.

My father, Adrian, once told me about how working for a dishonest lawyer for a short time in the 1940s made a big impact on his life. He only lasted eleven months, quitting when he found that his employer's gambling losses caused the man to use his client's money. A few months later this lawyer was forced to leave his practice and California. Eventually he was disbarred. Short-term, he was ahead, but dishonesty caught up with him and ruined his life.

Honesty has worked for me time and time again, and it will work for you. But let me say this: Being *absolutely* honest does not mean being *completely* honest. You don't necessarily have to offer damaging or negative information. You don't have to use honesty as an excuse to hurt people's feelings.

For instance, let's say I'm managing an act on a tour that is doing average business. I wouldn't open the conversation to a concert booker by saying, "By the way, we're not selling out anywhere." Instead I would pick the three cities where we were doing the worst business, and talk about them, getting it out up front, specifically calling attention to them, in effect, preempting the possibility of this information hurting a new deal. Then I'd talk about how well we're doing in many other cities. I haven't lied. Instead I have left a positive impression while still telling the truth and leaving other negatives unsaid.

THINGS GO BETTER WITH COKE ... UH-HUH!

On one occasion I was negotiating simultaneously with Pepsi and Coca-Cola, who were both bidding for Lionel Richie's endorsement. Our agent Jay Coleman approached Pepsi first and established a floor for the deal that approximated what he had negotiated for Michael Jackson the year before.

Then we heard murmuring of interest from Coca-Cola. Before I met with Coke, I let Pepsi know about the competition. I figured it would improve my bargaining position and avoid any impression that I was working behind their backs. "I'm not running off to make a deal with Coke, but I have to properly represent my client's interests, so I can't ignore Coke's inquiries," I told them.

When I got to Atlanta, I was just as open with the Coke people. "Look," I said. "We have a fine offer from Pepsi. We like the people there, and they got into the game early. I have to tell you that I think we're most likely to close this deal with them." Every word was true, and it made Coke come on all the stronger. I called Pepsi directly from the Coke offices and told them that things were heating up. They, of course, became concerned.

It was an enviable position, like having two suitors, each one becoming more determined as he discovers you might reject him for the other. In the end, we opted for Pepsi for all the reasons I'd mentioned to Coke.

Later, after the deal was done, a Coca-Cola executive called and asked me to spell out exactly why we had passed them up. I was very frank. "I know that Coke is the older, more established company, and I know you could have eventually matched Pepsi dollar for dollar, but the Pepsi folks took the initiative. They flew out and saw Lionel. They came to the table with a creative concept and a program, and they came first."

Most important, they made fast decisions and were seemingly not as bureaucratic as Coke. This gave them a real advantage in the negotiation process.

The Coke people understood, and by taking the time to clear up any misunderstandings I left the door open for other possible dealings with Coke in the future. In fact, my honestly paved the way for Coke's involvement in Hands Across America. (See the chapter on Negotiation.)

WOULD YOU HIRE THIS LADY?

One of my closest friends is Ralph Destino, the chairman of the board of Cartier in North America, who told me an excellent story about an acquaintance of his who was looking for a job.

She had been fired from her last job and had no solid letters of recommendation from former employers. At each interview, she danced around the subject, making excuses and trying to cover up the fact that she'd been fired.

Ralph suggested that concealing her past might be precisely what was doing her in. He advised her to walk into the next appointment with her head held up high, and take the offensive before the person on the other side of the desk could ask any questions at all.

At the next job interview, she just walked in, sat down, and the first words out of her mouth were "How do you do, Mr. Smith. Would you hire a woman who had been fired from her last job?"

The man was completely taken aback, but he was also impressed by her directness and honesty.

He hired her.

My feeling is that no matter how grim the facts may seem, you're better off telling the truth than struggling to cover them up. In most circumstances, honest mistakes are excusable. Deceit is not. When you're tempted to lie, recall Richard Nixon's actions during Watergate. Most political observers agree that his presidency would probably have survived had he come clean immediately and not attempted a cover-up. What ultimately brought him down was his attempt to keep the situation from the American public.

THE GREAT LATE-NIGHT WAR OF 1992

Clearly my reputation for honesty led me to the results I had with *The Tonight Show* incident, which in turn led to the end of the Arsenio Hall-Jay Leno late-night wars. What ended Helen Kushnick's reign as the show's executive producer was the fact that she was abusive and threatening to anyone who did not cave in to her tactics.

Travis Tritt was booked to do *The Arsenio Hall Show*, but the *Tonight* bookers kept calling me, asking for Travis to do *The Tonight Show* instead. They told me Helen was going to be "very upset." All of a sudden I got a call from Helen, and she says, "Arsenio is going in the toilet. You better pull Travis off Arsenio and put him on *The Tonight Show*. If you don't, he's never doing our show again." I told her that I didn't respond real well to threats. I soon found out that she had been doing the same kinds of things with everybody.

"You and I will be in this business for many years," Kushnick told me. "And we will never speak again. Travis Tritt will never do this show." Then she hung up.

My first thought after she slammed the phone down was "Oh no, what about Trisha Yearwood's upcoming date on *The Tonight Show*." And sure enough, within thirty minutes, Debbie Vickers, the producer of *The Tonight Show*, called to tell me that Trisha's date was canceled.

Now it just happened that the next call I received that day was from Robert Hilburn of the *Los Angeles Times*, and I said, "You can't believe what just took place. Trisha was thrown off *The Tonight Show* because I refused to cancel Travis's date on Arsenio." Bob told me that they had been hearing these stories for months but that no one would talk about them on the record. He asked me to go public with what had occurred. I figured, well, Kenny Rogers does Arsenio, Travis does Arsenio, and now Trisha's been thrown off *The Tonight Show*. What else can she do to me? These are my only three clients. Everyone said, "What a brave thing to do." But I had nothing to lose, and I wasn't about to let someone intimidate me.

And so, what did Helen Kushnick do next? She began trying to cover up, just like Nixon did, with lies to the media and excuses that wouldn't hold up.

A week later, Kushnick, despite having discovered Jay Leno in a comedy club at the beginning of his career and having Jay serve as the godfather to her daughter, was ousted unceremoniously from NBC, banned from the lot, and her professional relationship with Jay was ended.

I had no idea what a brouhaha it would be or that the woman would lose her job. I just believed that what she was doing was wrong. If I didn't have a reputation for being honest, it would have simply been my word against hers. All those years of building up my reputation for honesty paid off.

And I must say that Jay Leno really handled this situation well. He was either in the dark for many years or chose to ignore what people were saying about his manager, but once it all came to a head, he went out of his way to make sure that things like this never would happen again.

He called me personally, as he did other managers and publicists in town, apologized for the incident, and assured me that my clients would always be welcome on his show. And he's been true to his word: Both Travis and Trisha have appeared on *The Tonight Show* and *The Arsenio Hall Show* several times since, with no booking-war problems of any kind.

THAT ACHY BREAKY TRAVIS TRITT

Back in the summer of 1992, Travis Tritt caused something of a stir when he was asked what he thought of Billy Ray Cyrus's smash single, "Achy Breaky Heart." He responded that he didn't like the song. "If that's what country music is coming to," he said, "I'm uncomfortable with that. I didn't like the song when the Marcy Brothers did it, and I still don't like it."

Travis probably made a tactical error because the person asking the question was a reporter for the Associated Press, who walked out of the interview and immediately wrote a story about a big feud that was brewing between two of country's newest and most successful hunks—Travis and Billy Ray.

Most people said, "Why didn't he just shut up?" Well, he was asked a question, and he gave an honest answer. He didn't lie. He also didn't say anything bad about Billy Ray personally, nor did he set out to intentionally hurt him in any way.

I believe honesty was the correct policy and that everything happens for a good reason. This little media stir really helped to further define the Travis persona. I build images around people that are real. And real is what Travis is. He's an outspoken young guy who has opinions and is not afraid to give them. He tells you the truth. It works for him.

A few months later, at the Grammy Awards, Billy Ray did Travis one of the greatest favors in his life, standing there on national television and complaining about Travis's comments. Backstage, that's all the press wanted to talk about. You don't try to fight things like that, or muzzle the artists and say be nice to everybody. Travis doesn't like everybody. The more Billy Ray got upset about it, the more Travis had fun with it. But there are limits to everything. As of this writing, Billy Ray and Travis have had a very cordial conversation on the phone, and are making a sincere effort to bury the hachet.

THE HONEST RE-MARKETING OF KENNY ROGERS

For years, one of the strongest things Kenny Rogers had going for him was his all-American *family* image. He had the perfect-looking wife, a charming son, and was the ideal family man. The family even did commercials for Dole and Sterling Jewelry. It was an honest image built on the real facts of his life. But sometimes things change.

Having helped Kenny build a career based on this image, I had to shift focus in 1993 when Kenny's marriage broke up and his lifestyle became that of a bachelor. It meant that things had to be reorganized and redirected.

So what did we do? First of all, when the tabloids began writing nasty stories about Kenny's marriage troubles, he didn't hide from the truth. He came out honestly, admitted his mistakes, and told the truth. And that was that.

As we redirected Kenny's image, we began to emphasize the always-present and extensive charity side of his activities. This was the same approach taken by Michael Jordan when the media began to focus on stories about his gambling activities.

In Kenny's case, we also found that his appeal to women, which has always been his core audience, actually went up with his sudden availability.

We also began to put a considerable amount of emphasis on the TV side of his career. Fortunately he emerged as a first-rate actor while all of this was going on, maybe in part due to some of the inner turmoil he was going through. He seemed to be reaching inside of himself. His performance in the *Rio Diablo* TV movie with Travis Tritt and Naomi Judd was simply his best acting work to date.

In 1993 we put together a series of TV movies for Kenny to star in for NBC, playing a hotel detective named McShayne in Las Vegas. There's more edge to his character than there was before. And, for the first time, he can have a romance with somebody other than his horse.

KEY POINTS

1. TRUST. There is no more satisfying or effective career tool than honesty. Total, absolute honesty.
2. STRAIGHTFORWARD. You can get business to beat a path to your door by being the most honest person around. I've built an entire career on it, and think you can too.
3. INTEGRITY. A person needs only to catch you in a lie once to lose confidence and trust in you forever.
4. TACT. Being *absolutely* honest doesn't mean being *completely* honest. You don't necessarily have to offer damaging or negative information. You don't have to use honesty as an excuse to hurt people's feelings.
5. CANDOR. In an honest negotiation, the other side will be more willing to hear your point of view if you honestly spell out the positives *and* negatives of your position.

TIMING IS
EVERYTHING

*Never put off until tomorrow what
you can put off until the day after
tomorrow.*

—MILTON BERLE

Money manager Warren Buffett developed a sense of timing early in his life. He was just eleven years old when he bought three shares of Cities Service stock, which was then trading at 38. His fourteen-year-old sister followed his lead and bought three shares for herself, only to get cold feet when the stock slid down to 27. She badgered him about it so that when the stock rose up to 40, he sold all six shares simply to get her off his back. After making a net profit of $5, they watched the stock soar to 200. Buffett made up his mind then never to let anyone else influence him when he was sure of his judgment.

> **You can do the best work in the world, but if the timing isn't right, it's going to be wasted.**

Timing is a crucial element of career planning, but one with which Lionel Richie and I couldn't come to terms in 1986.

After "We Are the World," Lionel and I were discussing the next logical career step, and I suggested that we go after an Academy Award for one of his songs.

A few weeks later, director Taylor Hackford called me about his film *White Knights*. He asked about the possibility of getting a song from Lionel for the film. Lionel screened the movie and wrote the song "Say You, Say Me," for it. Motown released the song in October 1985 as a single, expecting it to be the kick-off single from Lionel's second solo album. His first album had sold an unprecedented fifteen million copies and produced several number-one singles. Unfortunately, this time the record company was going crazy. They wanted to have the album out at the same time as the single and the movie, but Lionel was hopelessly late finishing it. He had promised that it would be ready to be released with the "Say You, Say Me" single, but in reality, he was trying to finish two more songs for the record.

December came and "Say You, Say Me," was number one. In January it was still number one. February rolled around, and Lionel won a Grammy. Then in March, Lionel actually won the Academy Award for "Say You, Say Me." But still there was *no album*.

The record didn't finally get released until August. Lionel went through a number-one record that stayed on the charts, won a Grammy, had a *People* magazine cover and an Academy Award, but no new album.

When it was finally released, Lionel's album, *Dancing on the Ceiling*, had a few additional hits and sold 3.5 million copies, nowhere as well as the previous album, which had logged 78 weeks on the *Billboard* charts. Although the second album was a wonderfully crafted record, its sales disappointed everyone, especially Lionel.

"You've got to understand," I told Lionel, "that the extra three, four, five months you put on that album to get at least one more song that you liked perfectly were not as meaningful to the success of the project as your getting the album out at the right time."

Like I said, timing is everything.

TIMING AND NEGOTIATION

When I went to work in 1976 for the most successful manager of the seventies, Jerry Weintraub, at his Management III company, I learned an important lesson the hard way—by screwing up. I had never negotiated a salary before because I had always worked for myself. Consequently, I had no idea what my work was worth on an annual basis. So when he offered me $50,000, it sounded like a lot of money and I accepted.

After only a month I realized that I was working sixteen hours a day and that my contributions were worth far more than I was making. So I went back to Jerry and told him that we needed to renegotiate. Of course he didn't want to hear about increasing my pay scale. Instead he reduced my work load, in the process stripping away a lot of responsibilities that I really enjoyed. Not only didn't I get a raise but I lost some of the tasks that I really liked.

It was then that I learned an important lesson about timing.

> **Get your demands straight *before* you go into a negotiation because you don't always have a second chance. And be sure you've chosen the right time to make them.**

Timing is the ability to scout out opportunities and know when to seize or abandon them. Ultimately it comes down to a kind of sixth sense that lets you glimpse into the future. I went to Jerry to renegotiate way too early and ill prepared. But I did learn something.

STRIKE WHILE THE IRON'S HOT

After we finished *A Day in the Life of Country Music*, and delivered the show to CBS, everyone was ecstatic about the quality of the show. We began talks about doing a sequel, *A Day in the Life of Television*, and I knew the timing was right to go in and negotiate with the network for a pick-up right away. I felt it was important to do this before the show aired, because I knew that if *Day* did not rate well, they wouldn't be interested in a second project, even though, in reality, the two shows were quite different.

So I tried very hard to conclude a deal immediately, but CBS resisted. They wanted to wait and see how the first show did.

My instincts proved correct when *Day*, despite the finest reviews I've ever had on any program, got a very low rating (coincidentally, on CBS's worst night of the week—Friday). CBS passed on the sequel, saying the show's format was to blame, rather than its placement.

SONIC 2SDAY

After the crash of Atari in the 1980s, video games became generically known as simply Nintendo. Kids sat in front of their TVs for hours, sending plumbers Mario and Luigi into tunnels on the eight-bit Nintendo game system.

Then came Genesis and its superior sixteen-bit video game system, fueled by one of the fastest-moving and colorful video games of all time: Sonic, the Hedgehog, the spiky-haired, blue video-game hero.

Suddenly, video games didn't just belong to Nintendo anymore. So the Japanese powerhouse got on the sixteen-bit bandwagon with Super Nintendo in August 1991. It was now Sonic vs. the new sixteen-bit Mario Brothers game.

Sega, the creators of Sonic, knew they had to respond to Nintendo and that the response had to feature Sonic, their corporate mascot of sorts. The company video-game designers had a new Sonic game in the works, but they couldn't get it into stores until very late in the pre-Christmas selling season: November 24. But Sega didn't let that little piece of negative news deter them.

Sega put together a $10-million teaser advertising campaign, which kicked off in September with weekly promotional events leading up to a November 24 release date. It was dubbed Sonic 2sday.

Sega set up a "street date" strategy, similar to what was done in the recorded music industry, and which had never been tried before with video games. What Sega did was etch into every American kid's mind that November 24 meant one thing: Sonic 2sday.

Retailers, anxious to get holiday sales, were taking advance orders as fast as they could come in. By Sonic 2sday, in fact, some 400,000 copies of the new $50 video game had been presold. And on the first day of sale, an additional 600,000 cartridges flew off the shelves—an astounding million copies in one day!

Sega had further reason to pat themselves on the back: The Japan-based firm made Sonic 2sday a global event, with simultaneous promotions held in Europe and Japan. And by Christmas, worldwide sales of Sonic 2 had reached 4.5 million copies.

KNOW WHEN TO HOLD 'EM

Knowing when not to make a move, of course, is equally as important as knowing when to strike. If your company is going through financial belt-tightening, it's probably not the best time to ask for money for a new project.

I remember one time when I ignored this basic principle and almost paid for it. I was looking for funding for Hands Across America, and AT&T ("Reach Out and Touch Someone") seemed absolutely the perfect choice. I had a meeting with one of the top execs at AT&T, and he seemed extremely enthusiastic about the idea. I had ignored, however, the fact that the timing couldn't have been worse for AT&T to spend the $5 million we needed to help put our event on.

The government had forced AT&T to divest itself of certain interests, and as a result, the company had just laid off five thousand employees. We waited more than a month for their answer as our valuable organizing time slipped by. In the end, it was clear that, considering the current circumstances, they couldn't make the large expenditure we needed.

Fortunately, Coca-Cola came in to save the day. Look for the complete story in Strategy X: The Power of Giving.

KNOW WHEN TO FOLD 'EM

Although, as an entrepreneur, I'm a great advocate of taking risks, there are always times when the smartest thing to do is just to cut your losses.

This is often one of the hardest decisions to make if you're passionate about a project or an idea. Although I couldn't be more familiar with the line in Kenny Rogers's song "The Gambler," I had to learn when to fold 'em the hard way.

In the mid-eighties I became involved in financing and producing a wonderful musical *Lies and Legends*, based on the songs of the late Harry Chapin. This work was a labor of love for everyone involved—from director Sam Weisman (*Family Ties*, *Moonlighting*) to the cast, which included Amanda McBroom (*The Rose*), her husband, George Ball, and several other outstanding performers.

The show opened in Chicago at the Apollo Theater and received excellent notices. Nevertheless, as is typical with most regional theaters, it struggled to find a large enough audience to support its costs. However, I managed to convince myself that the show was so good that more advertising would do the trick. I had thrown more than $150,000 away before I realized that when you have something the public wants, you can't keep them away, and when, for whatever reason, they don't want it, no amount of advertising and promotion is going to work.

It is a lesson I have unfortunately learned several times in my career, when my passion for something has exceeded my good judgment. Knowing when to fold 'em is clearly an important part of learning how to use proper timing in your career and life.

KNOW WHEN TO WALK AWAY

Another example of when I walked away from something that for me became a losing proposition was when I folded my hand on the Burt Reynolds account in 1989. I had enjoyed a highly productive and fascinating eight-month relationship with Burt, one of the biggest stars I had ever represented. At the time, he was in the midst of making a major career comeback via his new starring role in *Evening Shade*, which would pay off a few short months later with an Emmy.

The downside, however, was that slowly but surely, my work for But had begun to take over my life, limiting the time I had for my other clients and my family. The tension that was being created was rapidly reaching a dangerous level. Part of the reason for this was Burt's own drive and passion for his career, which would see him working at all hours of the day and night on whatever particular project he was immersed in.

I finally came to the realization that despite the loss of hundreds of thousands of dollars in commissions, it was time to fold 'em.

Obviously, not everyone else is going to have the luxury that I had in being able to make that decision. Although the move might not cost you financially as much as it did me, you have to figure out what continuing the relationship is costing you physically and emotionally. I always find that if I make the right decision for my life, it turns out in the long run to be the right economical decision as well.

If you find yourself in a situation in the workplace similar to mine with Burt Reynolds, start looking around for something else. I'm not saying you should simply walk away from a very difficult situation, but I think there's always a way out. At the very least, you should start looking for viable alternatives instead of tolerating conditions that continue to make you miserable or unhappy.

HOW TO RUN FOR PRESIDENT

When we were doing the original *Smothers Brothers Comedy Hour*, writer Mason Williams came up with the brilliant idea of running Pat Paulsen for president.

At first, Mason wanted to run an object for president, like the Empire State Building, but then, after watching Pat do those hilarious editorials every week, he suggested trying to elect Pat instead.

The idea began as a fun joke on the show, but it ballooned into something much larger. *The Comedy Hour* satirized what was going on in American society each week, so Pat's campaign was a natural outgrowth of the approach of the show. We had all those great writers, like Steve Martin, Bob Einstein, and Rob Reiner, and political satire was what the show was all about.

Viewers loved it, and we sold CBS on the idea of doing a *Pat Paulsen for President* special.

Meanwhile, the campaign really took on a life of its own because we tapped into something current in America. The mood of the country was one of dissatisfaction with politics. After Robert Kennedy was shot, and the choice became Richard Nixon or Hubert Humphrey, people became very disillusioned with the electoral process.

Pat's campaign was good for him, it was good for the show, and it was good for America because it gave us all some well-needed comic relief from the tragic events of 1968.

Timing was key here, because we were able to capitalize on the mood of the times, just like we did later with "We Are the World" and Hands Across America. These moments are there, but they are short-lived. The key is realizing when to strike.

Pat went on to get two hundred thousand write-in votes, despite the fact that we went on the air the Sunday night before the election and urged viewers not to vote for him. (We feared that his votes might take away from the legitimate candidates.) The satirical campaign gave Pat an identity, and something to talk about every four years as he continues his try for the White House.

KEY POINTS

1. PUNCTUAL. Timing is a crucial element of career planning. You can do the best work in the world, but if the timing isn't right, it's going to be wasted.
2. MEASURES. Timing is the ability to scout out opportunities and know when to seize or abandon them. Ultimately it comes down to a kind of sixth sense that lets you glimpse into the future.
3. ABSTAIN. Knowing when not to make a move is equally as important as knowing when to strike.
4. DEUCES. As Kenny Rogers sings in *The Gambler,* "You've got to know when to hold 'em and when to fold 'em." Sometimes the smartest thing to do is simply to cut your losses.
5. EARLY. Get your demands straight before you go into a negotiation because you don't always have a second chance. And be sure you've chosen the right time to make your demands.

STRATEGY X
THE POWER OF GIVING

It is more blessed to give than

to receive.

—ACTS 20:3 5

At the start of World War I, Henry Ford sailed to Europe with a group of pacifists to try and persuade the leaders of the warring nations to call a cease-fire. When he returned, he conceded that he had not reached his idealistic goal, but he had learned something important.

"Russia," he said, "is going to be one hell of a market for tractors."

Ford sailed to Europe to do good and ended up doing well for himself and the Ford Motor Company. Giving is like that. Once you set out to do something for others, you find that you're on a two-way street and others, even inadvertently, will do good for you.

I believe the Power of Giving can bring you the greatest rewards in life, not just spiritually, but emotionally and materially as well.

> **I use charity heavily in what I do, because I believe you can enhance lives and careers (including your own) by giving to others. I can say personally that I've gotten more satisfaction from what I've done for people out of true generosity than anything else I've been involved with.**

I also believe any motivation to get people involved in charity is good. Make a conscious effort to apply the Power of Giving to your own career and you'll reap unexpected rewards.

For example, the Power of Giving is an excellent way of saying something about yourself to your employer. If you organize a charity event in your company, you've increased your visibility in a way that everybody wins.

However, I consistently find that the more altruistic your motive and approach is to charity work, the more you'll ultimately get back. The less you worry about what you are going to get out of it, the better off you'll ultimately be.

During my days of traveling to promote Hands Across America, I ran into a young airline steward who was anxious to know what he might do to help the hungry. He said he felt somewhat powerless because he was only a steward.

I countered that nothing is as powerful as a good idea and suggested he look at his own company and surroundings to find a way to help. "Why not," I said, "see what the airline is doing with the food left over after flights. Might it otherwise be shared with the community?"

He grabbed this idea and ran with it, eventually instituting a program through which the airline contributes its unused food to local community food banks. The airline reaped excellent publicity while doing good for a great number of people, and the steward received considerable recognition for his idea and the efforts he put in to seeing that it was executed properly. And as an added bonus, his company rewarded him for his efforts by promoting him.

YOU ALWAYS GET BACK MORE THAN YOU GIVE

I would say that perhaps the shining example of getting back more than you give happened to my wife, Cathy, and several of her girlfriends one Christmas.

They had decided to go caroling and chose to begin at the Veteran's Hospital in Los Angeles. They wandered into the building, but couldn't immediately find anyone to talk to. As they kept walking down the corridors, they were finally approached by a man in patient's garb, a man named Fritz.

The women explained to Fritz what they had come for, and he was obviously delighted. He promptly took them from room to room, acting as sort of an unofficial master of ceremonies, asking each patient what songs they'd like to hear, and sometimes even singing along with Cathy and her five friends.

As they began to go up to the top floor, the group ran into a hospital administrator who questioned why they were going up there. The patients on that floor were terminally ill, he said, and many of them could not even raise their heads.

Fritz dismissed this notion quickly saying, "The last thing to go is hearing. Come on!" Fritz and Cathy and the other women headed up to the floor with the very sick patients, and contrary to the administrator's opinion, the patients on this floor seemed to be most appreciative of all. True, many of them couldn't move, but on their faces the women could clearly see the effect of their visit and of the carols they were singing.

Later, as the women prepared to leave the hospital and were saying good-bye to Fritz, they discovered the most miraculous part of this evening. It seems that Fritz was to be operated on the next day for prostate cancer. That night he was very lonely and scared. He had gone to the hospital chapel to pray for something to get him through the night.

At the same moment in time the women were driving toward the hospital, themselves praying for a successful and meaningful experience. Fritz had six sisters, but they were all back home in North Carolina. Then he walked out of the chapel and ran right into the women. It was as if God had answered his prayers and sent his sisters to be with him!

Clearly everyone got much more from this night of giving than they had ever expected.

GIVING BACK

It's now a standard way of doing business for companies to contribute to charities. It's so common, in fact, that it hardly even gets any notice anymore. When Jerry Lewis announces the multimillions raised every year for his Labor Day Telethon, in fact, some 90 percent of it comes from corporate contributions.

One leader has been America's symbol to the world, the Golden Arches. When Ray Kroc opened his first McDonald's in 1955 in Des Plaines, Illinois, he started a then unheard of trend by giving back directly to the local communities with donations for schools, churches, and little leagues. He felt that if McDonald's took something out of a community, they also had the obligation to put something back in.

He saw it as an investment in the future. He saw it as good business. And he was right.

GIVING YOUR SERVICES

Early in your career when your own resources are meager, personal service is the most effective form of giving. Later, as you become more influential, you can share your expertise and lend personal support and praise to benefit colleagues and friends. All of these forms of giving are extremely valuable to others. Ironically, straight donations of money are often the least effective gifts of all because money is an impersonal commodity. To tap into the Power of Giving, your gifts must reflect your own personal qualities and talents.

I'd like to suggest some other imaginative ways to give:

• Give Time:

I have a friend who became a junior associate in a law firm. Eager to prove herself, she let her colleagues know that she was willing to accept extra casework when they were overloaded. Eventually, one of her associates became ill and asked her to take on two of his new cases. She found them far more challenging than her own, and they gave her an opportunity to practice a slightly different area of the law. She did a great job, and upon his return, her colleague praised her work and promised to send her more clients in the future. The rest of the firm began to view her as a competent team player and assigned her more challenging cases. Thus, she gained the recognition and experience to advance far more quickly than she could have if she had been less generous and worked solely on her own caseload. The kind of generosity that builds a career involves both responsibility and skill. Had the young lawyer approached her colleagues too eagerly or had she not been able to handle the more challenging casework, her "pushiness" could have damaged her career. As it turned out, she had enough self-awareness and understanding of her associates to make her actions work in her favor.

• Give Food:

Everybody loves to eat, and everybody loves getting an unexpected gift of food—even if they're on a diet. I had a student whose wife was a terrific baker, who brought fresh muffins to our class every week. As a result, he not only made a huge impression on me, but on the rest of the class as well. My first wife, Jinx, an author of cookbooks, used to make up baskets of food to give to friends at Christmastime. Each item in the basket (a loaf of bread, some cookies, homemade jam, etc.) had attached to it a little recipe card, so the recipients could make it themselves if they enjoyed it. This gift really captured the old-fashioned spirit of Christmas.

• Give Photos:

In this age of "Double Print Day" at most photo labs, another successful gift is a photo you've taken of someone. It's a great present for almost anyone, particularly people whose ego plays a major part in their lives—like perhaps your boss! People love photographs of themselves. Some of the nicest and most enthusiastic thank-yous I've ever received have been from celebrities to whom I've sent photographs of themselves. On the old *Smothers Brothers Comedy Hour*, for example, I kept a camera with me at all times, taking pictures, to document the guests' week with us. These were put into a leather-bound book and sent to them with a note. More than twenty-five years later, some of these stars still mention these books when I see them.

GIVING GIFTS AS A WAY OF LIFE

I've been sending out unique Kragen and Company felt wall calendars since the early 1960s. I've tried to quit a few times, but they're so popular and useful that people just won't let me stop. I believe in giving gifts that people will display in their home or office. Something they will be so proud of that they want to point to it, and say, "Look what Ken gave me." Or something so useful that they think they can't do without it, like my wall calendars. When you give something that has an ongoing life to it, that not only reaches the person but is a lasting reminder of your generosity, it's just good business.

We give to get back. That's what I do, day in and day out. I try to give with as much sincerity and lack of calculation as possible, and yet seemingly I always end up getting back more than I give. From a business standpoint, we give gifts to motivate people to work extra hard for us, to give us that extra ounce of effort necessary to make things happen successfully.

One important key to gift giving is knowing something about the person you're giving it to. Your giving is most effective when you either give something the person wants, or get something that clearly demonstrates you've put in a considerable amount of thought and effort into it.

For example, to help launch Trisha Yearwood's third album, *The Song Remembers When*, in 1993, we sent to radio-program directors five hundred personalized "talking frames," pictures of the album with a personalized phone-machine-type message with it. Each frame has a personal message along the lines of "Bill, I really appreciate all the support you've given me over the years, and I hope you enjoy my new album." The point here is that Trisha did every one of the messages personally. The more personalized you can get with these things, the better they'll be received.

FUN GIFTS

I've always believed in the fun of giving also. It's something we do as a truly enjoyable part of our business. One of my favorites was the time I came up with a really unusual gift for Mo Austin, the head of Warner Bros. Records. I went to an antique store, saw a commode (a toilet), with a flower bowl in a fancy piece of furniture that had come from an old ship. I bought it and put a gold plaque on it which read: TO MO. ANYONE WHO TAKES AS MUCH SHIT AS YOU OUGHT TO HAVE ONE OF THESE IN HIS OFFICE.

Mo kept it in his office for years, showing it to everyone who came to visit him. He got a real kick out of it, and it gave me much goodwill with Mo and the company.

For years, when I had a bigger company, I would go around spontaneously and hand out $100 bills to each of my employees whenever we would do really well. It was surprise giving that showed I would share our successes with those who helped attain them.

APPRECIATION

I can't tell you how few times in thirty-five years an artist has said to me, "Gosh, thanks, I appreciate what you've done for me." In fact, every time they've done that, I've gotten a high that's carried me for weeks.

Appreciation is the easiest, least expensive, and the most effective of all gifts. It's saying "thanks" in both gestures and words. That's the gift the recipient seldom forgets and values the most.

> **When you notice a person doing an outstanding job, write a short complimentary letter, note, or fax spelling out why you think the job was well done. Even better, address the note to the person's supervisor. Keep in mind that this technique becomes more, not less, powerful as your career advances.**

When I was putting together USA for Africa, I received a glowing note from Reverend Robert Schuller, whom I had never met. It simply said: "I've been watching what you're doing and I admire it. Keep up the good work." As the momentum built around our relief efforts, I received another note from him, this time saying, "Congratulations on the latest success. It's terrific."

I decided that I should give him a call; but when I phoned his office, his assistant told me he was on the road. "But I just got a note from him," I said. She explained that the reverend keeps a telephone dictating machine hooked up at all times so he can phone in these kinds of notes from wherever he may be. His office gets the letters out in the next day's mail. It's a tremendously effective and simple way to make new contacts and keep old ones "warm."

- If your boss or colleague gets married or his daughter graduates from college, send a note of congratulations.

- When an associate receives a promotion, bury whatever envy you may feel and offer your support. If you can remain an ally, you may move up the ladder together.

- By the same token, when a colleague gets fired or goes through some other setback, show your support. Help in any way you can. Eventually, people who are suffering misfortune today land back on their feet (it happens time and time again) and they tend to remember those who turned their backs on them and those who didn't.

GIVING FOR PUBLICITY

There's a reason why Jerry Lewis stays up for forty-eight hours every Labor Day weekend to run his telethon. Not only does he believe in the cause of raising money for multiple sclerosis research, it's also a way of keeping him in the public eye.

Bob Hope has kept his career alive since the 1940s by traveling abroad to do shows for the military. Not only does it give him something to talk about, but it's provided valuable material for his yearly TV specials. And, of course, he's done a lot of good bringing entertainment to the troops.

National patriotism is an obvious way to reach large numbers of Americans with a positive message. The only key to it, like everything else an artist does, is that it has to come sincerely from his or her own feelings, or sooner or later it will backfire. If you are doing it reluctantly, it shows in the long run.

I thought that when Clint Black and wife, Lisa Hartman Black, went to Somalia in 1993, it was brilliant. They were the first ones to go, and while it was a difficult trip, it gave them enormous visibility, and something to talk about when they came home.

It also happened conveniently just before the launch of Clint's new album and the start of his concert tour.

LIVE AID

The two-continent Live Aid concert in 1985 was one of the best examples of innovative giving in entertainment history. Organizer Bob Geldof's initial goal—and he succeeded—was to educate millions of people all over the world about hunger and persuade them to donate time and money.

But the concert's impact went beyond even that. It gave the performers an international platform beyond any they could have dreamed of, and it won Geldof a nomination for the Nobel Prize and eventual knighthood in Great Britain.

The concert was not designed with these objectives in mind, but there's no disputing the fact that the project was a milestone for charity efforts on a global scale, and a turning point in the careers of Geldof and many of the others who helped create this event.

The Live Aid example is particularly compelling because it was not designed by someone in the pinnacle of his career. When Bob Geldof was first inspired to do something for hunger relief, he was lead singer for the Boomtown Rats rock group, a midlevel group that had never really broken through. He had neither money nor much power within the entertainment industry. But he was tenaciously determined to make a difference nevertheless. He saw images of children starving in Africa on TV, he got angry, and then he got to work.

First he called on the music people he knew and asked them to participate in the 1984 Band Aid recording. He badgered and prodded people until they agreed. As a result of Bob's efforts, the record went on to earn more than $10 million for famine relief. Then he went after leaders in business, politics and the media, as well as musicians worldwide to help him make the Live Aid concert a reality. With unstoppable drive and energy, he organized this landmark event in less than six months.

"WE ARE THE WORLD"

After Harry Belafonte saw the film footage by African director Mohammed Amin of the horrible death and depravation in Ethiopia on the

NBC Nightly News, he became convinced that American artists should also be doing something for these people.

When he approached me with the idea of holding a musical event to support African famine relief, I honestly thought the project would be another charity event where you work hard, give the proceeds to a good cause, and go on with your life.

But even before the recording session for "We Are the World" was over, I knew that we had created the kind of "gift" that could make a real and lasting difference in the world and in the lives of everyone who participated.

"We Are the World" was an amazing experience. It inspired people all over the world to give generously and forced them to face up to the reality of what was happening to a large segment of the people on this earth. Millions were literally starving to death.

Belafonte's first idea was a concert, so he called New York promoter Ron Delsner. Ron, who knew I had managed the late hunger-activist/artist Harry Chapin, and was currently handling Lionel Richie, suggested calling me instead. I wasn't immediately encouraging. I had been trying to put a concert together for months to raise money for hunger in America, but had very little success getting artists to agree.

Instead, I said, let's take Bob Geldof's idea of Band Aid, an all-star recording session, and do a bigger version of it with American artists.

After I hung up, I immediately phoned Kenny Rogers, explaining to him my idea of an all-star recording to raise money. He said, "Count me in." Then I got into my car and drove over to Lionel Richie's house, where he and his then-wife, Brenda, were waiting for me to drive them to a meeting at Dick Clark's office. I explained to Lionel and Brenda my conversation with Harry. It turned out that they, too, had seen the NBC report and were looking for a way to do something about the tragedy in Africa. I suggested that Lionel write a song with Stevie Wonder, and that I would round up a dozen or so major stars to sing on the record.

For the next twenty-four hours, Lionel tried unsuccessfully to reach Stevie Wonder. Then, the following afternoon, Brenda Richie was shopping for Christmas gifts in a jewelry store when lo and behold, she was approached by Stevie Wonder, who asked for her help in choosing some gifts. "Not until you call my husband," said Brenda. "He's been looking for you."

They tracked Lionel down in a dentist's office, and Stevie agreed to write the song with him.

Meanwhile, I caught Quincy Jones as he was about to board a plane for his vacation in Hawaii. Quincy, who was totally overworked and about to begin producing his first movie project (*The Color Purple*) with Steven Spielberg, nevertheless agreed to produce the record. Furthermore, he suggested bringing Michael Jackson into the project.

When Lionel and Quincy contacted Michael, he not only wanted to sing on the record, but he wanted to help write the song as well.

So, within thirty-six hours I was able to call Belafonte back and tell him (with great satisfaction, I might add) that a song was being written by Lionel Richie, Stevie Wonder, and Michael Jackson, that it would be produced by Quincy Jones, and that I already had commitments from three of my other artists—Kenny Rogers, Kim Carnes, and Lindsay Buckingham—to sing on the record.

Harry couldn't believe it. Everything had moved so swiftly and perfectly. And yet the real work had only just begun. Over the next five weeks I spent every waking hour talking to managers, agents, artists, lawyers, record companies, publicists, and anyone and everyone who could help make "We Are the World" a success.

My goal was to get two artists a day to say yes. I figured that a total of fifteen was all I needed. I started at the top of the record charts and worked my way down.

However, once Jon Landau, Bruce Springsteen's manager, convinced him to join us, everybody wanted to do it. Before I knew it I had not fifteen artists, but twenty-eight. I decided to cut it off. Time was short and I was worried about all the logistics and clearances each artist required.

The number stayed at twenty-eight until three days before the session. Then Michael Jackson called me over the weekend and said he wanted several of his brothers and sisters to participate. Michael was playing such a key role that I couldn't say no. Then Quincy decided he needed some additional key voices, and brought in Dionne Warwick and several others. In twenty-four hours the group escalated from twenty-eight to forty-five. This was particularly embarrassing to me, since I had already turned down people like John Denver and Melissa Manchester, who very much wanted to be a part of the recording.

Joan Baez, for example, was furious with me, because she felt that as a long-time social activist, she should have been asked to participate. She was right. However, I was focused on selling records to raise as much money as possible, so I concentrated on the top artists *currently* on the charts.

Some people actually turned *us* down. These included David Lee Roth (his manager hung up on me!), Eddie Murphy, and even Barbra Streisand, who simply couldn't make up her mind on whether or not to do it.

Meanwhile, Lionel and Michael were once again having difficulties tracking down Stevie Wonder. He had disappeared. He'd gone off to Philadelphia and no one could find him. So Lionel sat down and wrote part of the melody and the lines "We are the world, we are the children." He put it on tape and took it to Michael, who listened with interest, and that night, went into the studio by himself and finished the music.

But there still weren't any lyrics, and in fact none were written until less than a week before the January 28 recording session when Quincy Jones laid down the law. He needed to be able to send the participating artists demos with lyrics so they could learn them before the night of the session. At that point, Michael and Lionel went to work and in less than two hours wrote the memorable lyrics to "We Are the World."

The next night was the demo session. As Michael and Lionel prepared to cut the demo, to everyone's surprise, in walked Stevie Wonder. He announced that he was there to help write the song. Michael and Lionel didn't quite know what to say—they had, of course, already finished it.

But finally they got up enough nerve to play it for Stevie, who listened intently, made one or two suggestions and then left as suddenly as he had arrived.

We stayed in the demo session until nearly 3 A.M. It was one of those private events that will always remain vividly in my memory. Michael and Lionel dancing and clowning together in the vocal booth while cutting a demo version that the public would never hear.

When the session was over, we all sat on the floor in the studio, carefully discussing plans for the actual recording session, which was now less than a week away. Quincy quickly proved why he was the perfect choice to produce this record. "We can't leave *anything up in the air* when we're in the studio," he advised. "Every artist needs to be told *exactly* what he or she is to sing; in fact, we should print it on the music so there can be no question. Otherwise, each artist will want to sing whatever they think is the best line and we'll have chaos. We also need to put tape down to show where each artist will stand, so no one can jockey for a better position."

Michael Jackson's tiny, high-pitched voice broke in. "Diana Ross doesn't like where she's standing." That remark really cracked us all up.

In order to decide which parts should be sung by which artists, arranger Tom Bahler took home recordings by each artist and listened carefully to their musical styles and vocal ranges. He then came back to Quincy with suggestions for the order and sequence of the voices. Quincy then modified this, and it was actually printed on the music.

To further ensure the absence of politics at the recording session, Quincy also hung up a sign: CHECK YOUR EGOS AT THE DOOR. He also sent that message to the artists in a letter with the demo tapes.

One person whose name made it onto the music, but who never showed at the session was Prince, who at the time was vying with Michael Jackson for the public's attention as the hottest artist of the year. We thought we might nab the elusive pop star because of the Sheila E.–Prince connection. Sheila E. was dating Prince at the time, and had toured extensively with Lionel. She had agreed to do "We Are the World," and Lionel and Brenda kept telling me that through Sheila E. we were going to get Prince. We were all so optimistic, we even put Prince's name on the sheet music, to give him a part to sing right after Michael Jackson's solo.

Prince's management kept saying he wasn't coming, so we probably shouldn't have jumped the gun. To Prince's credit, he did call during the recording session to offer to lay down a guitar track. But Quincy Jones politely declined, telling Prince that the tracks had already been cut five days before.

Anyway, along with many of the other artists who would record "We Are the World," Prince came to the American Music Awards that night. But unlike the others, who went afterwards to A&M Studios to record the song, Prince and two bodyguards went to Carlos N' Charlie's restaurant on the Sunset Strip. They left the place at 3 A.M., and one of the bodyguards punched out a photographer.

The next morning, the *Los Angeles Times* had a big story about the "We Are the World" sessions, with a sidebar box about Prince and his bodyguard inside the article. Prince unfortunately got a great deal of negative publicity out of that incident. What might have happened instead if he had joined the others? I must say, however, that Prince was the very first artist to donate an original, unreleased song for the *We Are the World* album, adding greatly to the sales of that product. And when Hands Across America came along, Prince again stepped up, contributing $10,000 for the cause.

While the "We Are the World" recording session was really an amazing experience, it almost didn't happen.

The night before the session, several of the rock performers who were to appear on the record decided they would pull out. The news was brought to me backstage at the American Music Awards rehearsal by Dave Wolff, who was Cyndi Lauper's manager and boyfriend.

He said that the rockers didn't care for the song and didn't particularly want to be associated with the nonrockers. There is a line from Lionel Richie that is appropriate here: "You are who you hug." The rockers clearly felt that if they stood on the same platform and sang with middle-of-the-road artists like Lionel, Kenny Rogers, Dionne Warwick, and others, it would affect their public image.

And so, not realizing the momentous event that was about to take place and feeling that even the song itself was too commercially oriented for rock purists, the rockers decided to bolt and run.

And yet the most important among them, Bruce Springsteen, held fast. He didn't care. He was going to be there and do what he could, no matter what. And in the end that's what held the rock community in place.

They all wanted to "hug" Springsteen, and if he wouldn't walk away with them, they recognized that they would look pretty stupid and self-serving.

Disaster was averted by the fact that one human being put the survival of millions of people above any personal consideration and lived up to the commitment he had made to participate.

The next night Bruce impressed me once again when he arrived at A&M Studios. Limousine after limousine had pulled into the security-protected confines of the studio grounds. Only Kenny Rogers and one or two others drove their own cars in. But Bruce went even one step further. Arriving at the airport himself, he rented a car and drove to the studio. I happened to walk out to the gate to see what was going on at that moment and through the crowd came Springsteen.

His first words to me were, "Man, I found a great parking place right across the street." He hadn't thought to drive his car into the studio, but simply parked, got out, and walked through the crowd.

* * *

"We Are the World" was put together in just thirty-eight days, which at the time, seemed like an impossible task; but in retrospect, it was perfect timing. I've found that some of the best things I've ever done have been put together in a very short period of time because everybody's focus is very intense and the energies high. When you have a long lead time, you tend to fritter the time away and decisions are put off. Deadlines force action, and with a shorter time frame, the media is generally still in their honeymoon phase with you and on your side.

Immediately following the recording session, we began meeting with leaders of the business community to come up with other pioneering ways we could work together to help feed the hungry.

When and how did the song grow from simply a charity record into a movement? How did we turn a song into more than a single event? Interestingly, that was done for us by two radio DJs, independently deciding that it would be wonderful if all the stations in America played the record at the same time on Good Friday.

While the DJs were the ones who came up with the idea, we helped them put it together. We took their concept and turned it into a real event by concentrating everything we were doing to happen in the same time period. MTV devoted Saturday and Sunday to "We Are the World" and HBO ran a two-hour special on the making of the record and video. So once again, we had an event with threes—radio, MTV, and HBO.

The week after the recording session, I went to New York City and had the one truly religious experience of my life. I felt that Harry Chapin had entered my body.

After seeing the twelve-page layout that *Life* magazine had prepared, I was driving away when I had this overwhelming feeling that Harry was inside of me, and he was directing everything I was doing. Suddenly I became the doer of his will. It was one of the things that pushed me to keep going. Another was a letter I received from a twelve-year-old girl.

She said that her parents told her not to send the money, because it wouldn't get to the starving kids in Africa, but that she was sending her allowance anyway. Twelve cents in coins were taped to the letter. I felt I had an obligation to that little girl and every person who had sent in money to see that their faith could do good and would be fulfilled. I felt that if we let them down, they might never again feel it was worthwhile to contribute to charitable causes.

And so, what had started out as a simple charity event became virtually a way of life, a full-time occupation. In order to keep my own business going as well, I had to add eight to ten hours to my work day, and I had to spend considerable amounts of my own money on my charity work.

At the same time, my own career took new and exciting turns in very practical ways that I could have never predicted at the outset. In the space of one year, I received more public recognition, more high-powered contacts, more professional respect, and more personal gratification than I'd achieved in all my years in the entertainment business. The experience not only made me realize the power of giving, but it made me see that everyone can use this age-old concept to improve their personal and professional lifes.

HANDS ACROSS AMERICA

Hands Across America was announced in October 1985 and put together between the following January and May. By Memorial Day, 1986, we had convinced five and a half million people to stand holding hands in a line that spanned 4,152 miles through seventeen states.

Frankly, it would have been far more difficult to make a success of a standard benefit march or concert than to pull together Hands. When I first mentioned the idea to people, their reaction was, "That's fantastic," and then in the next breath, they'd ask, "But that's impossible. How are you ever going to pull it off?" I couldn't answer, but I knew that somehow we would make it happen. And it wouldn't require nearly as much agonizing as would a minor event. The excitement surrounding the idea would force it into reality. Working big is easier than working small because everybody gets a charge out of doing the impossible. You get more help, more interest, and more attention.

Hands began as a natural outgrowth to "We Are the World." A very creative man named Jeff Nightingale was consulting on publicity for us. One night, at intermission of a "We Are the World" benefit performance by the New York City Ballet, he looked at me, and said, "Don't laugh—what would you think if we strung people from the

Atlantic Ocean to the Pacific Ocean, and they held hands and sang 'We Are the World'?" I said, "I'm not laughing. It's just impossible enough to be possible."

Then I went off to Africa and forgot all about it.

A month later, I returned and was picked up at the airport by a volunteer. As we were walking through the terminal, he said, "It's wonderful what you're doing for Africa, but when are we going to do something for America?" An imaginary light bulb truly went on in my head right there—Hands Across America.

Since AT&T's campaign slogan was "Reach out and touch someone," I approached Ma Bell about sponsoring the event, but the idea got bogged down in their bureaucracy and budget cutbacks.

Fortunately, I ended up with Coca-Cola. I called Coke exec Sergio Zyman and explained the project in three minutes, adding that we needed anywhere from $3 to $5 million to make it happen. "You've got it," Sergio said, right then and there. As I said, people are turned on by the seemingly impossible.

This was September and we were looking at doing the event in May.

As we were starting to put together Hands, the USA for Africa board was discussing how the proceeds would be spent. I felt strongly that 100 percent of the Hands money go to America. The board resisted. Some members argued that as much as 50 percent should be earmarked for Africa, since that was the organization's original objective. Others suggested a split that favored America, with only 10 percent going overseas. I held out because I sensed that the success of this event depended on a clear-cut theme: American money for Americans. If we confused the issue by making it "America for Americans and other people too," we would not get the solid national support we needed. Eventually my convictions won the board over, giving Hands the solid patriotic undercurrent it never could have had if the money had been split. (By the way, 10 percent of the "We Are the World" moneys also stayed in the U.S.A., thanks to Stevie Wonder, who suggested this at the recording session.)

The feeling while putting on Hands Across America was one of enormous excitement. But it was also really scary—I'd fly across the U.S.A. and see miles and miles of land, and say, "How will we ever get people to fill all that space?" Finally, we made a rule that none of our staff could take window seats on flights.

Putting on Hands Across America was just like being in politics.

I'd give speech after speech, TV interview after TV interview, go to three or four cities a day to stir up the volunteers. I'd exist on about two or three hours of sleep a night.

And just like "We Are the World," Hands also almost didn't happen.

With less than two months to go before the May 25, 1986, event, we had fewer than a million people signed up for a line we knew would take a minimum of five million people to complete. The media stood poised to pronounce us a failure even before the day of the event. Furthermore, we had no insurance.

My friend Peter Ueberroth had assured me that the Olympic Torch Run had come off without a hitch. It took eighty-two days and it, too, went from one end of the country to the other. Still, our lawyers and insurance agents predicted disaster. The board of directors of USA for Africa were in no mood to let the event go on without the proper insurance, and in fact, most of the municipalities we would go through were insisting upon it.

We were told that for every two hundred thousand participants we could expect one death or injury.

Of course, it was true that we were asking millions of people to stand in the street in the middle of the day, in the desert heat or midwestern rain on Memorial Day weekend, one of America's worst weekends for death on the highways.

Since nothing like this had ever been tried, who knew what might come of it?

To make matters worse, America was in the grip of an insurance crisis of major proportions. The very week that the board insisted we finally had to get insurance or stop the event, there was a *Time* magazine cover story on this crisis, detailing all the events and activities that had to be curtailed as a result of lack of insurance. The cover headline: SORRY AMERICA, YOUR INSURANCE HAS BEEN CANCELED.

With the board's ultimatum that I had to have insurance within twenty-four hours or stop the event, I went off to New York on the all-night "red-eye" flight. Not knowing quite how I would pull it off, but believing that there must be a way, I checked into the Plaza Hotel at 7 A.M., hoping to get some rest before my 11:30 A.M. meeting with the man who was my last remaining hope for insurance.

No sooner had I fallen soundly asleep than a jackhammer in the hallway awakened me.

I opened my door to find that the Plaza was tearing down the opposite side of the hallway. There was nothing but rubble and rocks where I had walked a half hour previously. Even worse, my protests resulted in the construction workers throwing pieces of plaster at me as I stood half-naked in the doorway.

I went back to my room and sat down, thinking things couldn't possibly get any worse. And then I suddenly remembered that someone had told me the head of the insurance company was a big fan of Kenny Rogers. Somewhat in desperation I hunted Kenny down by phone and asked him to call the president of the insurance company and do the best selling job of his life.

I waited tensely for the next half hour until Kenny's return call. He finally came through with good news. He had reached the insurance man and somehow—amazingly—extracted a promise that by the time I left the meeting that day I would have the insurance in hand.

What the man hadn't bothered to tell Kenny was that it would cost us *Three Million Dollars*! This was an incredibly steep figure. Even with the pledge from Coca-Cola, we only had seven or eight million dollars in the bank with which to promote the entire event. (We had estimated that the event would cost between $18 and $20 million total—*without* the insurance. And we eventually came in under budget at $17 million including insurance.)

Still, if we had no insurance, we had no event, so we had no choice. Needless to say the insurance company walked away with an enormous profit—but they had provided us with what we needed when no one else would do it. This allowed five and half million Americans to band together on the 4,152-mile chain on Memorial Day, holding hands and sending a spectacular message about America's commitment to solving the problems of the hungry and homeless.

POSTMORTEM

What can we learn from these events and the problems and the hurdles that had to be overcome?

First of all, you can see that both events came close to not happening. Thornton Wilder said it best: "Every great thing in the world balances at all times on the razor edge of disaster." I've thought of that many times as I've worked my way through the difficulties that always seem to arise when you're trying to do anything of significance.

"We Are the World" and Hands Across America taught me to never say anything is impossible.

• You Have to Believe in the Ultimate Success of What You're Doing.

In almost every major personal, business, or charitable endeavor in my life, there have been moments where I could easily have thrown in the towel if I hadn't believed strongly. That faith is critical to any undertaking. Perhaps Albert Schweitzer said it best in a quote I often used during Hands Across America: "We must become good plowmen. Hope is the prerequisite of plowing. What sort of farmer plows the furrow in the autumn but has no hope for the spring. So, too, we accomplish nothing without hope. Without a sure inner hope that a new age is about to dawn. Hope is strength. The energy in the world is equal to the hope in it. And even if only a few people share such hopes, a power is created which nothing can hold down—it inevitably spreads to others."

• The Public Will Respond If You Give Them Something Unique, Innovative, and Meaningful to Respond To.

They're just waiting there, anxious to participate.

I didn't do anything so tremendously significant with "We Are the World" or Hands Across America. I simply recognized the opportunities that existed as Americans tried to respond to the horrible pictures out of Africa of women and children dying—and later, to the strong feeling that hunger and homelessness must not be allowed to continue in the richest nation in the world.

The success of Hands Across America created so much momentum. Had we been more thoughtful about how to follow up, we could have made much more headway. But the event was so overwhelming just to get on, and so fraught with the threat of failure, that no one could focus on anything else.

We missed an opportunity by not having a follow-up. But we did send a message to Congress. Hands Across America clearly got the government's attention. And it got the media turned on to the issues. Still, had we taken the additional steps to plan the follow-up better, who knows? Perhaps some kind of permanent national agency might have been formed to deal with the issues of hunger and homelessness.

THE THREE BASIC RULES OF GIVING

Rule 1: Give 'Em More

One of my business philosophies is to constantly give people more than they expect in every area I deal in. For instance, when Kenny Rogers's solo career first took off, the concert-industry norm was for there to be a superstar headliner and an opening act. So Kenny's promoter C. K. Spurlock and I packaged three acts together and gave them all equal billing. By packaging three artists instead of just two together and treating them all as stars, we gave people a show that was stronger than what they usually got for the price of one ticket. This made it an imperative ticket for them to buy, and turned the show into an event.

The perceived value was greater than people expected.

When Kenny put out his first greatest-hits album, the industry norm was to include four or five legitimate hits and about six filler songs. What we did instead was to take *ten* legitimate hits and put them on one album. Then, again to do something that had not been done before, we added two brand-new songs. One of the new tunes was the Lionel Richie composition, "Lady," which became Kenny's biggest solo hit. This new material gave radio something current to play, and that in turn pushed the album.

The record sold fifteen million copies, the biggest-selling record of the 1980s until it was surpassed by Michael Jackson's "Thriller."

My good friend Jeff Pollack uses this philosophy every day in his business. Jeff is a radio consultant, and he believes there's more to a successful radio station than just hit records and entertaining DJs. Jeff's company specializes in creating great national promotions to create local interest. For example, he organized stations in 1990 to celebrate what would have been John Lennon's fiftieth birthday by simultaneously playing "Imagine." He helped get stations involved in Earth Day, as well as raising money for the Walden Woods project and earthquake victims.

"No one asked us to do those things," he says. "They expected us to just consult on the music and work with the on-air talent. But we just feel that by creating new ideas that haven't been asked for, we enhance the value of the relationship."

Rule II: Give to Increase Business

Hard as it may seem to believe today, in 1980 eighteen of the National Basketball Association's twenty-three teams were losing money, and four were close to going out of business altogether. Turned off by high salaries and widespread drug use, basketball fans barely filled half the seats in the arenas. Television wasn't interested. The NBA championships weren't even broadcast live on network television.

David Stern changed all of that, with the Power of Giving.

Named commissioner of the NBA in 1984, the former NBA general counsel was given a mandate to save the NBA from self-destruction. He controlled the players' salaries and cleaned up their image, and was able to increase the average attendance from ten thousand per game to seventeen thousand in 1993.

And why would basketball players agree to a drug program, a public service program, and salary caps? The Power of Giving. Stern convinced the NBA team owners to give the players 53 percent of the league's revenues from tickets; network, local, and cable television; radio and all international TV that is broadcast live. He threw in a cut of the royalties from sales of licensed NBA team products—a huge business. And he encouraged the players to become active in a variety of social services and charities, and heavily publicized and promoted this activity.

So, in other words, Stern made the players his partners by giving them a major piece of the pie, and watched as basketball exploded in the eighties, with superstars like Magic Johnson and Larry Bird.

And thanks to the Power of Giving, everybody won.

Another good example comes courtesy of Starbucks, the hot gourmet-coffee retailer that's been popping up on trendy street corners as fast as McDonald's did across the street from malls in the seventies and eighties.

To make sure coffee drinkers who come in to sip mocha java and other exotic brews don't leave Starbucks without a bag under their arm, the company created a frequent-buyer "passport" program. You not only get a free half-pound of coffee for every ten half-pounds purchased, but they also added incentives for trying each of Starbucks's more than thirty coffee varieties.

Rule III. Give to Your Own Career

I don't care what business you're in, you won't make it unless you're willing to invest in your career. A small business needs to advertise to bring in customers; a job seeker needs to spend money on a professional-looking resume and attire. *You need to spend money to make money* or get attention.

After recording his *Can't Slow Down* album, for instance, Lionel Richie wanted to produce a really splashy video for his song "All Night Long." Music videos were a relatively new phenomenon (the song actually predates Michael Jackson's "Billie Jean" by a few months) and he saw "All Night Long" as a perfect song to be used in a video with lots of production and dancing.

Motown would only advance us its normal $35,000 (remember, this was the early days of video); yet the video was going to cost us more like $250,000 to produce. Lionel and I felt we must find a way to do it. So he simply underwrote the project himself. In the end, we were able to recoup the money through the sales of home videos, and the video became such a hit that it truly advanced all areas of Lionel's career. It increased record and concert sales and positioned him in the forefront of the new medium of music video.

Then there was the time that Kenny Rogers finally landed an eight-week contract as headliner for the Riviera Hotel. He felt like he'd made it, but I quickly took the wind out of his sails by suggesting that he hand over to me his entire first week's salary of $75,000.

With the $75,000, I bought billboards in Los Angeles and Las Vegas, covered the cabs in Vegas with ads, and made badges for the hotel employees to publicize the engagement.

In the local papers we ran a full-page letter from Kenny thanking the people of Las Vegas for their support over the years and inviting them to the show. We hit the local radio and TV stations with the same message.

The blitz worked. Before we were through, everyone in town was talking about Kenny Rogers. In a matter of days those three weeks were sold out and we bought another full-page ad headlined THANKS/ SORRY. In it we thanked everyone for supporting Kenny and told those who'd been turned away that Kenny would be back in May, five months later. As a result of that ad, the May date was sold out by the end of January, an unprecedented event.

The Riviera, recognizing a good thing, tore up his initial contract and handed him a new one, extending the run to twelve weeks instead of eight and raising his weekly rate to $135,000. That's more than a $1-million difference. I'd say spending the initial $75,000 more than paid off.

DRESSING FOR SUCCESS

One last thought: It's one of the oldest techniques in the world, but it works. You really have a much better chance of impressing people if you dress well. Nobody wants to work with a slob.

McDonald's Dick Starmann tells me that when he began with the company in 1972 he didn't have much money, but he felt it very important to show that he was ready for the corporate world by dressing for the part.

Once a year, he would go to Brooks Brothers to buy a new suit. "I could go somewhere else and buy two, but I felt strongly that I'd rather have one good suit, and build up my wardrobe slowly rather than have two suits that didn't look as good," he says. "When I started with McDonald's, I was in advertising, and I felt like I was representing the company to the outside world, so this was really my uniform. I bought the suits with my own money, but I saw it as an investment in my career, an expense of being in the business world.

"Wearing Brooks Brothers suits today probably doesn't mean as much as it did back then, but I think the same message is still important. Looking good pays off. Not only dressing well, but looking healthy and feeling healthy. We all know that when people look good, they feel good, and perform well."

You may be only your company's runner, but every time you make a delivery you're meeting a potential contact for the future. The impression you make on just one person can change your career and even your life. It all starts with the way you look and dress.

KEY POINTS

1. GENEROSITY. You can enhance lives and careers (including your own) by giving to others. I've gotten more satisfaction from what I've done for people out of true generosity than anything else I've been involved with.
2. ATTENTION. The Power of Giving is an excellent way of saying something about yourself to your employer.
3. ILLUSTRATIONS. There are many ways to give and get ahead in business—gifts, appreciation, and time are three obvious examples that will pay off.
4. SINCERE. The more altruistic your motive and approach is to charity work, the more you'll ultimately get back. The less you worry about what you're going to get out of it, the better off you'll be.
5. PROFIT. You may not always gain in material ways, but when you add up the emotional rewards of giving you'll *always* get back more than you give.

NEGOTIATION

*The secret of managing is to
keep the guys who hate you
away from the guys who are
undecided.*

—CASEY STENGEL

Not long ago I met with the senior vice president of a major film company who kept repeating every other sentence out of my mouth and asking the same question over and over again. On the surface he seemed eager to work with me, but it was obvious that something was out of whack, so I scuttled my planned presentation and shifted the conversation to his side.

Through a few casual questions I found that a new CEO had just come on board that week. Although he didn't come out and say it, I could see that he was afraid for his job. He wasn't about to approve any new projects until the chief had shown his stripes.

Once I discovered what was bothering the man, I knew it was pointless for me to make my pitch at this time. So I used the rest of the meeting to find out more about him and the changes in the company.

Several weeks later, after things there had shaken out and he felt secure again, I returned and successfully closed the deal.

One of the most important tools in negotiation is knowing how to read people. In negotiation or out of it, whether you are dealing with a demanding boss, a troubled employee, a hostile competitor, a nervous client, or a dissatisfied partner, it will always help your position if you understand why the other person feels the way he or she does. It doesn't require a sixth sense or a master's degree in psychology. Just watch and listen to other people carefully. Put yourself in their position. See yourself on their team, and look at the world through their eyes before you pass judgment or take action of your own. Not only will this help you map a successful strategy for dealing with them, but they will be more responsive to you.

I believe that it's almost always better to negotiate in person rather than over the phone. On the phone, your cues are restricted to tone of voice and choice of words. Face to face you have a broad spectrum of psychological indicators to draw on: body language, facial expressions, gestures, attention span, dress, and general mood. Singularly or taken together, these can tell you how hard a bargain the person is willing to drive. For example, if it's impossible to hold his gaze, you'll probably have a harder time coming to terms than if he looks you straight in the eye.

Casual conversation at the start of an important business meeting can provide you with valuable information about the session to come. You'll be able to tell if someone is in a particularly surly mood that day, which may make reasoning impossible. You may spot signs that the other side is overly eager to please, which you can use to your advantage. Preliminary chitchat lets you sniff out who the real leaders and followers are on the opposing team. These roles don't always correlate to corporate titles. Sometimes people spill out neutral information in these warm-up periods, which you can use in future meetings. Remembering personal details like the name of a spouse, the number of children in the family, a favorite restaurant, or sport can win you several important points in the next encounter.

Some other tips:

• Seeing the Other Person's Point of View:

One thing I like to do in any negotiation is to negotiate from "the same side of the table" physically, or if that's not possible, then mentally. This concept—detailed in Roger Fisher and William Uri's *Getting to Yes*—is to try and see the issue from the point of view of the person you're negotiating with, to see what his or her needs, problems, and objectives are in this negotiation, and in turn for him or her to see what your objectives are. You can put the other person at ease by asking the kinds of questions that allow you to understand what that person's position is, and by offering information that shows why you're behind your position. It's the quickest way to get to a successful negotiation, and I do it every day.

• Honesty:

I often offer pieces of information that clearly are not in my own best interests. This raises my credibility with the other party, which in turn gives credibility to what I'm asking for. It always seems the more honest I am, the more successful the negotiation. (For examples, see Strategy VIII: Absolute Honesty Is the Best Gimmick.)

• The Middleman:

Whenever possible, I like to be once removed from the negotiating process. In fact, I very often use a lawyer (a deal maker, not a deal breaker) to act as the person to put forward the major points. This allows me time to think about my responses. It also allows my lawyer to say, "I don't think he'd be willing to consider that." It's a technique that's often very effective because it's much easier for the middleman to play the bad guy, and it gives you an opportunity to come back with a compromise and not blow the deal.

• The Going-Over the-Head Theory:

My days are usually spent solving problems, getting people who have said no to change it to a yes. To think of ways to make something happen when everyone is saying it can't happen. A while back Trisha Yearwood wanted to shoot a video at the Ryman Auditorium in Nashville, but we were given an absolute no from the man who ran the historic old hall. He said he had had numerous bad experiences with film crews. However, the Ryman location was important to Trisha's video, so I refused to accept the no. Instead I went to his boss, with whom I had excellent relations. I asked if he could intercede. He said he didn't like to pre-empt his employee's decisions, but he'd see what he could do. Fortunately, the no turned to a yes; we filmed Trisha's video at Ryman Auditorium and the man who had originally turned us down couldn't have been nicer or more helpful once we got there.

With a situation like this, you have to be careful. You don't want to go over someone's head in a way that alienates them. So you look for an opening. When he says, "I'm sorry, they won't let me do that here," you say, "Would you mind if *I* gave them a ring to see if I can possibly change that?" That way, you're not sneaking around someone's back but doing it with their blessing.

• The Timing-Is-Everything Theory of Negotiation:

When you're trying to get somebody to buy something from you, you've got to know when to strike. For instance, when we wanted to sell Travis Tritt's life story to New York book publishers, we waited to pitch the project until Travis was playing Radio City Music Hall in New York City, home base to most major publishers. We waited for the perfect time, a week when a lot of things were happening for Travis in New York. And we made the sale.

• The Enthusiastic Negotiation:

I use enthusiasm in everything I do, and that includes negotiation. I believe that if I'm enthusiastic about what I represent, the other person will be more likely to make the deal. This was certainly the case when I got Coca-Cola's Sergio Zyman to put up $5 million to make Hands Across America happen. My proposal, to some, could have seemed crazy, but I was so enthusiastic I actually convinced Sergio I could pull off this seemingly impossible idea.

NO SCREAMING PLEASE!!!

I know a manager of a very hot recording act who suffers from a problem that is too rampant in my business: He loses his temper way too often. He is constantly concerned that his client isn't receiving everything he deserves, despite the fact that his client is actually doing very well.

As a result, this manager is always berating people for not giving his client his due, and he alienates people every day. The results are self-fulfilling, because people don't want to deal with him. Who wants to be yelled at?

People might have a different feeling about him if he took a more relaxed, less hostile approach. The point here is that negativism reinforces itself, the same way positive optimism does.

I believe CBS's then-president Bob Wood canceled *The Smothers Brothers Comedy Hour* at least in part because he was unwilling to argue with Tommy Smothers.

The content of the show and the mood of the sixties was such that CBS representatives were always objecting to things in the program. My then-partner, Ken Fritz, and I would always try to handle CBS's objections calmly and keep Tom and Dick out of it. We acted as buffers.

But by the beginning of 1969 both Ken and I were gone, and Tommy began dealing with CBS directly. His problems with the network were real and often justified, but unfortunately the end result was usually some heated argument.

The show was no longer number one (it had slipped to number seventeen), and was not as critical to the network's ratings as it had been in its first two seasons. Tommy may disagree with this (we're good friends now), but I believe one reason CBS canceled the show was because they just didn't want to deal with the hassles anymore. It was easier for them to eliminate the show, thereby getting rid of the source of irritation. They also avoided potential embarrassment with the new Nixon administration, which was just coming into power and had it out for the networks.

The lesson is that moderation would probably have served the Smothers brothers better. You can get a lot more from people by taking a conciliatory approach. I believe Roseanne Arnold will learn the consequences of this one day. When you're on top, nobody will balk, but the minute your position weakens, it's a whole different ball game.

HOW TO KEEP YOUR COOL

No one gets through life without making a few enemies. But not everyone who blocks our career goals is actually against us. They may simply have different agendas. If we're smart, we'll minimize friction and place ourselves psychologically on the same side of the table so that we understand the other person's point of view. Some tips on how to do that:

1. Determine Who's at Fault.

In the heat of an argument, it's easy to accuse the wrong person. It's even easier to shirk your own share of the blame. Once the dust settles you'll probably feel apologetic and more than a little embarrassed, but by then the damage is done. The person you've wronged may never speak to you again.

The best way to avoid this trap is to step back from the situation as soon as you feel hostility brewing. Call in an impartial observer if necessary to help you identify the source of the problem and the critical issues. Remember that personal disputes rarely flow in one direction, and you may deserve at least some of the blame. If so, try to see through your anger and irritation. Purely emotional reactions will only undermine your negotiating position in the long run.

2. Act, but Never React.

The point here is to be as calm and conciliatory as you can be with your adversary. This is exactly how I responded to Helen Kushnick when she threatened to keep my clients from ever appearing again on *The Tonight Show*. I didn't yell, I didn't scream, I just spoke to her calmly, and said that I didn't respond well to threats.

My advice is to become increasingly calm the more things heat up. This at the very least gives the impression that you are in control of the situation. Study your opponent, listen closely to his or her arguments, and look for clues in his behavior and emotions that may help you resolve the conflict. This information will give you the winning advantage.

Remember, the other negotiators almost always have a good reason for how they're reacting or what they've done—right or wrong. Try to understand their perspective on it.

3. Use Reverse Psychology.

Reverse psychology provides the basis for a fruitful compromise. Even if you're negotiating with your spouse over a vacation plan, try to understand his or her point of view before you state your position. Start by listing all the points on which you agree. Make requests, not demands. Stand your ground on the issues that matter most to you, and give in easily on the incidentals. Above all, don't pressure people into a decision and then try to rationalize that it's what they really wanted all along. Find a solution the other person agrees to voluntarily.

4. Look for Opportunities for Alliance.

Even archenemies can become allies given the appropriate circumstances. It happens in politics; it happens in business. Given an overriding common goal, strong leaders will bury their disagreements in order to benefit from their combined strength.

When locked in disagreement, look for opportunities to work as equal partners toward a goal both of you can live with.

5. Keep in Touch Even If All Else Fails.

Although it may be the last thing in the world you want to do at the time, keep talking. Stay in touch with the other person and even the most dramatic blowup will eventually fall into perspective. If you don't, the misunderstanding may escalate to all-out war. Use whatever excuse you have to, but keep the lines of communication open.

THE ASSERTIVE NEGOTIATION

In the middle of the Depression, Babe Ruth's ball club asked him to take a salary cut. When he held out for his $80,000 contract, the club owner pointed out that he was asking to be paid more than Hoover made as president. "Sure," replied the Babe, "but I had a better year."

The best way to go into a negotiation is to be upbeat, positive, and assertive. To get what you want you have to substantiate your demands by telling your opponent exactly why you or your project is worth more. Your experience, your abilities, and your reputation are what really count.

SOLVING DISPUTES

Negotiation is generally thought of as cutting a deal, but it's also frequently being a mediator. Trying to come up with a solution that will make all parties happy. I see the negotiator's role as much like that of a parent who mediates feuds between children or establishes household rules. In my line of work, situations constantly arise where there are many different opinions about how a task should be done, as well as budgetary constraints, which limit how it can be done, and policy and time considerations, which determine how it must be done.

I often must negotiate all points of view at the table, weigh them against the objective facts, and come up with a compromise solution that will leave everyone feeling like a winner.

Whenever you make a major decision or settle a dispute, you need first to fully distill all the relevant information.

Steve Wynn of The Mirage once told me the techniques he uses to solve these kinds of problems.

1. Know Who the Players Are.

Sometimes the most powerful people in a negotiation or the most dangerous in a dispute are the ones who keep the lowest profile. You can't afford to ignore them. Always find out ahead of time who will be affected by the final decision and whose consent is needed to make that decision stick.

2. Take Time with Each Individual.

Having targeted the players, give each one equal time and allow enough time to hear each one out. Look at all sides dispassionately before you even think about your own position.

3. Maintain Your Own Neutrality.

If you take a stand up front, you're bound to alienate someone. Make it clear to everyone that you will not take sides until you've heard from each of them.

4. Do Your Own Research.

It's never a good idea to rely solely on secondhand information or personal opinions. You have to do your own homework. Go to the library, check the dates and numbers you've been given. Make the necessary calculations to fill in any blanks or gaps in your own data. Chances are you may see a solution that escaped the others.

5. Give Yourself a Chance to Think Alone.

After you're finished doing the basic legwork, go off by yourself to make up your mind. Take your phone off the hook. Leave the office. Do whatever you have to do in order to think clearly.

6. Don't Respond Until You Know the Answer.

Talk yourself through all the available options and don't make up your mind until you get the magic *click* that tells you you're right. As you gain experience negotiating, you'll be able to recognize the *click* more easily. If it doesn't come, don't take a stand. Present your honest opinion and explain why you feel hung up on the issue, but only commit yourself if you have a firm position.

While all the managerial roles require a certain amount of objectivity, the role of negotiator demands that you put your subjective concerns firmly into perspective. You must analyze your own position as ruthlessly as you tear others' apart, and if your position is weak, admit it.

KEY POINTS

1. ABSORB. Know how to read people. In negotiation or out of it, it will always help your position if you understand why the other person feels the way he or she does. Look at the world through the other person's eyes. This will help you map a successful strategy for dealing with that person, and he or she will be more responsive to you.
2. LIVE. It's almost better to negotiate in person rather than over the phone. Face-to-face you have a broad spectrum of psychological indicators to draw on—which can tell you how hard a bargain the person is willing to drive.
3. TRUTH. Negotiate honestly—offer pieces of information that are clearly not in your own best interests. This will raise your credibility with the other party, and give more credibility to what you're asking for.
4. INTERMEDIARY. Try to be once removed from the negotiating process if you can. Use a middleman like a lawyer, because it's easier for the middleman to play the bad guy. It also gives you an opportunity to come back with a compromise and not blow the deal.
5. ZEAL. Be enthusiastic. If you believe in what you represent, the other person will be more likely to want to make the deal.

PUBLICITY

When a dog bites a man, that is
not news. . . . But if a man bites a
dog, that is news.

— J O H N   B .   B O G A R T

Shortly before Harry Chapin's death in 1981, he gave me a piece of advice that was to become the cornerstone for the activities of USA for Africa four years later.

Kenny Rogers had instructed me to ask Harry what he'd do if Kenny gave him $1 million to fight world hunger.

"There's plenty of food in the world," Harry told me. "That's not the problem. Distribution is the problem. And that is controlled by the world's governments. People move the government, and the media moves the people. If you bought $1 million worth of food right now, you wouldn't even feed all the hungry in the world for one day. But if you applied the same $1 million to mobilize the media, you could start to change the world." So Kenny took the $1 million and set up the World Hunger Media Awards to reward and encourage the media to cover these issues.

I'm a big believer in getting your message out through the media.

Like it or not, publicity is a mandatory component of any career. When I say publicity, you may think of singers, actors, or sports figures. But in corporate life, successful people get publicity all of the time. The same, of course, goes for politicians, doctors, lawyers, and most other professions.

> **The actual definition of publicity, according to Webster's, is "any information or action that brings a person, cause, etc. to public notice." It's getting your message out there, and it's a critical factor in any kind of career advancement. In fact, it's important as well in personal relationships. You've got to get somebody's attention before you can even ask them out.**

Almost everybody nowadays has a story of some kind to tell. You don't have to be a high-level professional or axe murderer to find something interesting in your life or career worth promoting. With the advent of reality television, and proliferation of talk shows, the media is looking for interesting stories about real people every day. Don't wait for them to call you. Take the initiative and pick up the phone. And don't forget about your company newsletter, high school or college bulletin, local community newspaper, and cable TV public access channel.

The fact is, much of what we do on a day-to-day basis at Kragen and Company involves some form of publicity. First we do the work and then we tell people about it. When an actor works for me in a TV movie, I tell him that the acting is only half the job. The other half is publicizing it.

People in the public eye constantly need new projects to give them something to talk to the media about. That's one of the reasons why Travis Tritt costarred in the TV movie *Rio Diablo*. It gave Travis something fresh to promote.

But again, publicity isn't only applicable to show business. You could be doing the finest work in your company and if nobody knows it, you're never going to get ahead. To advance in any facet of life, you need to find ways to get recognition for what you're accomplishing.

If you just finished a great new report or project, don't simply rely on the presentation of the work to make an impact for you.

HOW TO GET PUBLICITY

The first and most important point about publicity is: What is it for? Why? Publicity without a purpose is meaningless. For me, publicity is a tool to gain some objective, and it needs to be coordinated with solid activity.

The key to getting publicity is to understand what motivates the media. They are looking for a hook. They have to have a reason to write or cover your story. If you're trying to promote a concept, a project, yourself, whatever, there has to be something that's unique, different, or interesting. The first thing you need to do is look for those kinds of things.

Of course, if you're looking at publicity on a regular, ongoing basis, you may want to consider employing a publicist. If you can afford it, it never hurts to have professional assistance. Again, this is the kind of investment in your career that can be important.

Publicists deal with the media every day, and the good ones know the keys to unlocking the doors that the media gatekeepers may keep closed to you. But just like anything else in your career, you can't simply turn the job of getting publicity over to a publicist. My experience has taught me that a publicist's work is only as good as the input you give him or her. You need to work closely and continually to ensure that the message they're giving out is the one in fact that you're trying to convey. They need to understand thoroughly what you're trying to accomplish by getting publicity. To do this, you yourself need to learn some of the rules of media managing.

1. Find Real News Value in What You're Pitching.

What's unique about your story? Is there a human-interest angle? Newspapers and magazines are always looking for stories that tie into a holiday period. Do you have a new Valentine's Day, Mother's Day, Christmas, or Thanksgiving angle for them?

2. Find a One- or Two-Sentence Phrase That Can Sell Your Story.

Reporters are very busy, and are usually writing or reporting a story when you call them. Needless to say, they're also usually on deadline. When you call to pitch, you should have practiced your story idea on several of your friends, letting them play devil's advocate to give you every reason why it isn't good. That way, you'll be ready for the toughest audience you'll have to face, one in which you'll be given ten to twenty seconds to make your pitch.

I produced a TV special called *A Day in the Life of Country Music*, a TV version of the book series which is exactly what it says it is: a day in the life of country music. Our pitch: twenty-two crews in twenty-five cities in twenty-four hours, filming forty artists. One sentence tells it all and says it's a unique, improbable, and newsworthy event.

FAVORITE ANGLES

Here are some angles that media outlets seem to always respond to:

• Success (or Failure):
If your record, movie, or business is thriving, that's copy. And, if there's something unusual about the sucess or failure, if it's the first time it's happened this way, or if you've broken some kind of a record, that's even more certain to spark interest. Look for the unusual angle that makes your success special, and you're likely to get the coverage.

• Celebrity Packaging:
Celebrities can often add cachet to an event. This works best, however, when the celebrity has some real reason for being involved. If you're staging an AIDS benefit and the celebrity's brother has died of AIDS, or if the celebrity came from the same small town as your event, you are far more likely to have credibility with the media. On the other hand, just having a celebrity involved can bring more people to the event, and hence, more media interest.

Nowadays, the biggest news is often made by celebrities dating or marrying (or divorcing) other celebrities. Couples like Julia Roberts and Lyle Lovett; Lisa Hartman and Clint Black; Burt Reynolds and Loni Anderson all experienced big career boosts when they got together. And in Loni Anderson's case, Burt's surprise filing for divorce unfortunately probably added substantially to her career stature.

• Conflict:
It is the essence of drama and the media loves it. Steve Wynn and Don King; Donald Trump and Steve Wynn; Mayor Ed Koch and

Donald Trump; Travis Tritt and Billy Ray Cyrus; Coke and Pepsi; Kellogg's and General Mills; General Motors and Ford; Mars and Hershey; David Letterman and NBC; Arsenio Hall and Jay Leno; even (for a few minutes) Ken Kragen and Helen Kushnick. She and I were major news despite the fact that neither of us were really celebrities, and both of our careers were affected. I'm normally a noncombative person and never would suggest you unnecessarily pick a fight. However, if you're in the middle of a media war of words, you may be able to turn it to your considerable advantage.

• David and Goliath:

The little guy winning against impossible odds is perhaps the biggest story of them all. MCI successfully took on AT&T. In the computer business, to receive favorable coverage, all you have to do is say you're competing with industry monolith Microsoft and the media will respond. Whatever it is that *you are* can be turned to your advantage. Avis did it by saying "We're only number two, but we try harder."

• Charitable Causes:

This is particularly interesting to the media at certain times of the year. Obviously Thanksgiving and Christmas are two times when the media looks for stories with heartwarming, "spirit of the season" angles. However, since the mid-eighties, there has been such a saturation of charitable events, that even these once surefire story hooks have become harder to sell. So even the best charitable event needs to have a fresh angle to it to attract publicity. What doesn't work is what's been done before. What does work is what's fresh and exciting.

MY BEST AND WORST PR STUNTS

The Doo-Dah Gang was really a stunt from beginning to end. The brainchild of director Bob Graham, the gang was a group of actors who pretended they were from the 1920s, just as if they had been taken by a time machine into the 1970s. They were perfect for Las Vegas, where I helped create a show for them at the Flamingo Hilton.

We kicked the show off with perhaps the greatest PR stunt I've been involved in. We flew the gang to Las Vegas in an antique airplane, and they were followed by a rival gang shooting machine guns at them from another old plane. When both planes landed in Las Vegas, there was a big shootout on the landing field. Then the Doo-Dah Gang jumped into their 1920s cars and raced to the Las Vegas Hilton, carrying a suitcase of phony money. They walked into the hotel, switched suitcases (unnoticed) with a member of the hotel staff. Now they had a suitcase with a real $1 million in it. With the media closely following them the gang marched into Hilton president Henri Lewin's office, dumped the million on his desk, said they wanted to buy the Flamingo, and that this was their down payment. Then they left for the Flamingo, and a week later we kicked off their show.

From A to Z, every step of the "event" was carefully planned to be true to the 1920s period, and the media ate it up. They had fun, and felt like they were in a time machine. The event paid off with wonderful stories, including a full-page article in *Time* magazine.

My worst PR stunt seemed like a good idea at the time, but it's one that just backfired.

My former client Dean Scott was booked to play the Playboy Club in Los Angeles, and we wanted to make a big deal out of the date. He was playing Easter weekend, so I hired some of the Playboy bunnies to personally deliver show invitations—along with live rabbits—to various VIPs.

Everyone loved having these beautiful women stop by their office, and they thought the real bunnies were very cute. The only problem was that now they had to feed the bunnies and find a place for them to live. It created more trouble than I had initially foreseen. People didn't want to be bothered with dealing with the bunnies. This was one stunt I definitely would *not* repeat.

PRESS CONFERENCES

One thing CEOs seem to love to do is to call their head of communications and order up a press conference. Sometimes the assistant doesn't have the nerve to tell his or her boss that the announcement doesn't warrant a press conference—the press might not show up.

But if you have a newsworthy event, as I believe we did with the announcements of "We Are the World" and Hands Across America, then by all means, call a press conference. Sometimes the press conference can itself be an event. But you have to have something that is truly special to make the press want to cover it.

Remember, they may already have interviews set up for the day, or some competing news story or news conference to cover. If your story isn't truly important or interesting, they may feel so burned that you'll get no press at all.

Sometimes, faxing over a release first thing in the morning (the earlier the better) and making yourself or your executives available can be just as effective for print coverage. Remember that for TV coverage, crews need something to photograph. Make a press conference as visually appealing as possible.

HOW TO MANAGE PUBLICITY

As the spokesman for Hands Across America, I learned a lot more about how the media works than I'd ever known as a manager working on publicity campaigns for clients.

I began the process by taking professional instruction. It taught me that the media will almost always try to *use you for their purposes*. The trick is to *use them* for yours. But first you have to decide your exact purpose, and then be sure your objectives are fulfilled in each and every interview you do.

I learned that you can't get more than two or three ideas across in any one session with the media. They have a story to report and it needs to be focused. The day of the wide-ranging interview is pretty much over. Most news outlets want bite-sized news stories. It's easier for them—and their editors—to focus on one to three ideas.

Pick the ideas that you most want to get out and no matter where the interviewer tries to take you, you need to lead things back to emphasize those points. Some politicians are incredibly skillful at that. They'll always find a way to say, "Yes, that may be true, but what's really important here is . . . "

In my training, I was taught to not evade the question, but to answer and lead right back to the point I wanted to make. Most important, I refused to allow the press person to impose his or her agenda on me.

MY WORST INTERVIEW

That prize goes to *The Plain Dealer* of Cleveland during Hands Across America. The reporter began by asking a series of questions that were all loaded with negatives. "Why is your overhead so high? Why has it taken you so long to get the money out?" and things like that.

The fact that our overhead was low and the money was going out faster and more efficiently than most charities didn't matter to her even when I said so. It was very clear from talking to her that she had an agenda. She was trying to get quotes for a story she had already planned in her mind.

After it was over, I called Marty Rogol, the executive director of USA for Africa, and told him that I had just experienced the most negative interview of my life. Then I made a big mistake. I said to him, "It's only in the *Cleveland Plain Dealer*. No one outside of Cleveland will see it."

Wrong! The media reads and watches itself all the time, and some of the lazier members of the media simply write stories based on what some other reporter has already done, never even checking to see if the facts in the first story are correct.

One person writes a negative story, and then another major newspaper or magazine picks that story up and treats it as if it's gospel.

A few days after *The Plain Dealer* article came out, I went to New York to do some interviews for Hands Across America. It was as if everybody in New York had read the article. That's all they wanted to talk about. They were quoting all the negatives from the story as factual.

Again: Never assume that one piece, no matter where it is, is unimportant. Once it's in print, it can haunt you and live on forever.

MEDIA TIPS

• **Think about exactly what message you want to get across.**
Remember that very little of what you say will be used.

• The person interviewing you is another human being.
It doesn't hurt to strike up a rapport or friendship. Tell the person honestly what you're trying to accomplish, and he or she might help you with that.

• If you experience negative vibes during an interview, talk to the person and try to turn it around.
What I should have said to the reporter from *The Plain Dealer* was this: "You already have a story in your head and a point of view that just isn't correct. So I'm going to stop the interview now." That's one way; the other is to try and convert them to understanding the damage their negative—and inaccurate—story could do.

You have to remember that often the media's agenda is different from yours. Sometimes they're not just attempting to write the most factual story, but writing to enhance *their own careers*, by unearthing something, or trying to make it sensational. These individuals can have enormous power over your success or failure, especially if they're with a major paper. One such person did exactly that to USA for Africa.

HOW TO DEAL WITH NEGATIVE PRESS

Dennis McDougal used to work at the *Los Angeles Times*, where his beat was music coverage. Then he was assigned to cover the role of Hollywood in charities. At first, he really made a difference with USA for Africa, helping us build momentum with some very positive stories. But then, much to our dismay, Dennis abruptly changed direction and appeared to be trying to uncover something that simply wasn't there.

Our goals were basically selfless and good: to raise money to combat hunger and homelessness. But Dennis apparently felt we were just too good to be true. He kept trying to unearth negatives. When he couldn't find them, he would either create them or imply things in a series of very negative articles. Because he was associated with such a powerful newspaper, he eventually brought a lot of our activities to a screeching halt.

I believe that Dennis McDougal was largely responsible for killing the movement that we began. The reason: Our board members were happy to volunteer their time, but they weren't about to let their reputations get damaged. And Dennis's stories were forcing our executives and board to constantly defend themselves.

We tried just about everything to stop him. First I tried talking to Dennis as a human being, explaining what his articles were doing to us. I'll never forget what he told me. "Ken," he said, "if the story has a real hook to it, it will be on page one. If it doesn't, it ends up on page sixteen. Wouldn't you rather be on page one?"

Not if the information was damaging and/or inaccurate.

His strongest attack was that we weren't moving quickly enough to distribute the funds raised by Hands Across America and "We Are the World." Our position was that we could get the money out fast, or get it out right. We had a limited amount of dollars to work with and we wanted to be sure they made a difference.

Besides, we were getting money out faster than comparable charities. But Dennis didn't seem to have any experience with charities to know this and apparently didn't attempt to find these things out.

Next, we decided to be really nice to him, We thought that if we let him spend a lot of time with us, he would see how good a job we were doing. But that didn't work either. He took the inside information he got and twisted it.

Then we tried going to his superiors with elaborately documented comparisons between his stories and those in other papers. We showed them the enormous bias and overweighted negatives in Dennis's stories. While they agreed, they took no action. They refused to reassign the beat to another more charitywise reporter.

So finally we did the only thing we could do. We closed him out. We stopped speaking to him. We froze him out of everything we did. Slowly but surely his stories dried up. He had no access and no hook.

The media is a very necessary watchdog, but in this particular case, an entertainment reporter was assigned to cover a charity organization because of the celebrity connection, and his lack of knowledge of charity work allowed him to take this misguided approach.

What did I learn from all of this? The real lesson is the power of the media to not only report on, but to shape events. Throughout these efforts I often told members of the media that they were the most important people in determining the success of our effort and that we wanted them to be our partners in this humanitarian undertaking.

The USA for Africa staff often admonished me for suggesting this partnership to the media (they felt we would be seen by the press as trying to co-opt them). But nevertheless, the majority of the media did indeed become partners in our efforts, and helped ensure that we succeeded.

My personal view has always been that, first and foremost, members of the media are people who want just as much as you and I do to make a difference in this world. Therefore, they can be appealed to on that level. Unfortunately, this didn't work in the case of Dennis McDougal.

THOUGHTS ON FAME

It took me quite awhile to physically recover from "We Are the World" and Hands Across America, and a couple of years to get away from the celebrity part of it. It was nice to have the proverbial fifteen minutes of national recognition, and then have it be over and return to a somewhat normal life.

After the Hands experience, I said to myself, "What does this celebrity and fame and recognition add to my life? What does it give me?" I decided that I could be happier and equally effective as a lesser-known person working behind the scenes.

The final nail in the coffin came from a brief mention of me in *Spy* magazine. It was one of their little lists, under the heading, "The Sixteen Things Hollywood Fears the Most." Number one was superagent Mike Ovitz. A few notches down was "Anything with Ken Kragen's return address on it." I figured that if I'd reached a point where there are some people who think if they get something from me, they're automatically going to be asked to contribute, then I've lost my effectiveness. Even if it isn't true, it could become a reality. Bob Geldof became a person who people ran away from. At Harry Chapin's funeral, Bruce Springsteen talked about how Harry used to berate him for hours about how he should be more involved in charity, and how Bruce would hide whenever he saw Harry coming. Bruce said it in a cute way, but I didn't want to become that. It was time to get back to business.

KEY POINTS

1. BROADCAST. Publicity is a mandatory component of any career. It's getting your message out there, a critical factor to any kind of career advancement.
2. RECOGNITION. Publicity isn't only applicable to show biz. You could be doing the finest work in your company and if nobody knows it, you're never going to get ahead.
3. SEXY. The key to getting publicity is understanding what motivates the media. They are looking for a hook. If you're trying to promote something, there has to be something about it that's unique, different, or interesting.
4. SHORT. In pitching your story to the media, come up with a good angle, and capsulize it down to one sentence. Reporters are usually on deadline, and you'll need to get their attention very quickly.
5. INFLUENCE. Recognize that the media has its own needs and agenda. Also, don't underestimate the power of the media to shape events and occasionally to change fiction into fact.

CAREERS

A career is a job that has gone
on too long.

—CARTOONIST JEFF MACNELLY

Frank Sinatra has had probably the greatest career in show business. He's successfully stayed at the top—doing things his way—longer than anyone else. But when I look for a career model from which to learn the triumphs and failures, I always seem to come back to Robin Williams. His has been the one career I would have most liked to have been responsible for. He has a broader range of talents and abilities than anyone else I can think of in the entertainment field.

Comedians have always had the most options because they can do their live stand-up acts, and they often become very good actors. Acting skill seems to be one component of the ability to be a good comedian. As a result, comedians usually have the option of doing TV or movies.

In Robin's case, as he recently proved as the voice of the genie in the movie *Aladdin*, he can also sing, and do so in several different voices. I'm truly awestruck by his ability to act dramatically in a film like *Awakenings* and then be outrageous and silly in a film like *The Fisher King*.

Robin is incredibly versatile and has a career that appears to have been built on the sheer quality of the work, rather than simply a large amount of celebrity.

And on top of all that, he believes in giving back. Every year, since 1987, he, Billy Crystal, and Whoopi Goldberg continue to host their Comic Relief telethons for the homeless.

So what can we learn from Robin Williams's fascinating career? No matter how much talent you have, it's ultimately hard work that is the key to success. In Robin's case, he proved he would do anything and everything to keep honing his skills. This dedicated focus and competitive quality is a constant that I see in virtually every one of the top stars I have come in contact with, including most of the superstars in business.

Few ever make it without a lot of effort, and certainly no one stays on top for long without it. Diversity is another quality to the career of Robin Williams; it's the same thing that has kept stars like Kenny Rogers and Steve Wynn successful for so many years.

STEVE WYNN: THE EVENT THEORY IN BUSINESS

When I think of great business careers, Steve Wynn's is at the top of the list. The chairman of the Las Vegas based Mirage Resorts, he's the ultimate risk taker. At a time when nobody was building new hotels in Vegas, Steve—whose empire then included just the Golden Nugget in downtown Vegas—had this radical idea that a family-oriented, theme-parklike hotel on the Vegas Strip would attract both high and low rollers and change the perception of the city.

His competitors called him crazy, but he made his hotel into an event, signing up Siegfried & Roy as the main attraction, installing a manmade volcano out front that erupts every fifteen minutes, housing live dolphins and white tigers, and eventually offering shows by the Cirque de Soleil as well.

He didn't just build a new hotel, but because he's such a stronger mover than shaker, he created the whole trend of Las Vegas as a family attraction. Even something as simple as putting an aquarium behind the check-in desk serves a purpose. It entertains people waiting on line, giving them something to look at.

Steve could have simply been content with having the number-one downtown hotel. He didn't have to build The Mirage, but the entrepreneurial drive within him wouldn't let him sit still.

The opening of The Mirage was a big event, with more than just three components. He took five different things—the opening of a new-style hotel, Siegfried and Roy moving to The Mirage with a five-year $57.5-million contract, dolphins and aquariums, the volcano, and a radical new Vegas policy, which said that you had to buy reserved seats for his showroom—you no longer had to slip $100 or $200 into the maître d's hands to get a choice seat.

He built all of those elements into the opening to make sure he gathered everyone's attention. And then, in 1993, when he opened up his new pirate-themed mega resort, Treasure Island at The Mirage, he pulled off another stunning mega event.

Here's the setup: Steve had bought the old Dunes hotel, across the street from Caesars Palace, and planned to gut it and begin building a new, modern showplace on the site in 1994. To publicize the opening of Treasure Island, which features live pirate battles in front, he staged a big cannon blast. The ball supposedly flew over Caesars Palace and Flamingo Boulevard and knocked down the Dunes in thirty seconds, footage that was aired on TV stations everywhere that night.

But wait, there's more. Steve created an entire TV movie around the event to air on NBC a few months later. Steve got James V. Hart, the cowriter of *Bram Stoker's Dracula* and *Hook* to pen a tale of a family who comes to vacation in Las Vegas and ends up rubbing elbows with Long John Silver and hidden treasures. Steve bought the time himself, for $1.7 million, and had the one-hour movie—or I should say, infomercial built around the blast footage—produced on his terms. This, however, was the movie that would live on forever. Steve plays it in The Mirage and Treasure Island hotel rooms hourly on closed circuit TV.

When I look at Steve's career, there are certain traits that stand out as good examples for all. First, as I said, he has the guts to take risks. He's willing to lead the way rather than to follow, and takes chances on new approaches with a sure, inner belief that he can pull things off. Next, he always goes first class. Right from the start, when he just had the Golden Nugget, he turned it into a first-class hotel in downtown Las Vegas, a neighborhood that had been known more for its glitter than glamour. Business promptly beat a path to his door.

Steve is also the quintessential business-showman, with a healthy mixture of P. T. Barnum and J. P. Morgan. He's willing to spend money to make money, and he leads. He never does anything halfway, and despite the fact that he has a super support team, he stays involved in almost every detail that's important to him.

GALLAGHER: HE COULD'A BEEN A CONTENDER

I believe that the comedian Gallagher could have been another Robin Williams. The level of Gallagher's comedic talent is probably on par with Robin's.

What has kept my former client from getting to the very top? Let's take a close look. Gallagher chose to stay small and very successful within certain limitations. He didn't want to be the world's biggest star. Instead he wanted a career that would service his life. And in Gallagher's case, this meant keeping control of all facets of it.

He felt he needed to do everything himself to feel comfortable, and that put immediate restrictions on what he could accomplish. He also never was happy with too many things happening at one time. He needed to focus on one idea. That often prevented us from using The Event Strategy, since it operates on three things happening in a short, concentrated period.

I first met Gallagher when I took Bill Medley to perform on the old *Mike Douglas Show*. Gallagher was on that show, and I thought he was as brilliant as anyone I'd ever seen. I approached him afterward to tell him how terrific he was, and to see if he would be interested in management.

He was immediately standoffish, and said he didn't need a manager. I handed him my card anyway, suggested he check around town to see what people thought of me, and left.

I then began to invite him to various functions we had at the company—the opening of new offices, a Las Vegas junket for Kenny Rogers, etc. Eventually he was knocking on my door for management.

My wife and I took Gallagher to lunch, where he trashed everything about the business. It was clear he had opinions about everything, and there was very little he liked.

As we walked away, Cathy said, "Well, I guess you're not going to manage him." And I replied, "I think I am, because he's a comedic genius." I've often found that there's a dark and difficult side to most comedians, and the extent of it is somewhat proportional to the amount of real talent involved. It seems the unusual way they look at life is both their greatest asset and liability.

So I began to work for Gallagher. He was already successful playing clubs, but I believed there was much more there to be had. I signed him in 1980 and put him on the bill with Kenny Rogers at the Riviera Hotel in Las Vegas. The man who became best known for crushing watermelons was literally a smash. Immediately I got him all kinds of great deals. Within a month, I had generated more money for Gallagher than he had made in the previous five years.

Besides the one hundred concert dates with Kenny (at $3,500 a night), I also got him a $100,000 record deal with Capitol Records, and then set my sights on television, where I truly believed that, in the Mork and Mindy era, he could be the next Robin Williams.

I called Gary Nardino (then the head of Paramount Television) and Bud Grant (then CBS Entertainment president), borrowed Kenny's plane and flew them to the Riviera Hotel in Las Vegas to see Gallagher.

I dropped the two of them off in the lobby while I went upstairs to change. When I came back down thirty minutes later, I couldn't find them. I eventually ran into Bud and Gary in the casino. They both looked somewhat perplexed. It seems they had run into Gallagher shortly after I went upstairs, and he proceeded to tell them how much he hated television, and why TV was such a bad medium.

"So why are we here?" asked Bud.

They both wanted to leave on the spot, but I pleaded with them to at least see his performance. When he was finished, they stood up, put out their hands, and said we had a $200,000 development deal for a TV series. They were drawn in by the same incredible talent that I was.

Suddenly, Gallagher was hot. We developed a TV series about a congressman from Idaho. The incumbent dies, and Gallagher is appointed to take his place, arriving in Congress on roller skates. It was called *Our Man in the House.*

Gallagher went to Washington to research the part and came back to L.A. in time to go with me to a meeting at CBS. He sat down and said to Bud Grant: "I'm sorry, but I can't do this. It would take me two years of research just to know what to do on the show." Then he walked out the door.

After the aborted attempt at the CBS project, I arranged for Gallagher to do his first special for Showtime. He left me shortly thereafter, but he's gone on to make an excellent career through his specials and live performances.

He seems to be happy not being the world's biggest star, but earning a good and steady living and having total control of everything to do with his life. He even books and produces his own shows, and has complete creative freedom. I'm still a big fan. Very simply, he really makes me laugh.

MICHAEL JORDAN: YOUR LIFE IS NOT YOUR CAREER

The career of the former Chicago Bulls superstar is fascinating to look at, particularly his 1993 decision to walk away from it all at the very peak. Clearly Michael made a decision that his career was no longer servicing his life, and that the things that were the most important to him could be best achieved outside of basketball.

Whether or not this decision holds, it's a fascinating one to see being made at this level. What will prove fascinating is how Michael will now service the competitive side of his nature. Maybe golf will take up the slack, or perhaps baseball, but clearly, Michael Jordan has a need to be a winner at whatever he does, and it's unlikely he'll remain idle.

MILTON HERSHEY: YOU CAN'T TAKE IT WITH YOU

Milton S. Hershey founded the American candy bar in 1894. By the end of his life in 1948 he had amassed a personal fortune worth $60 million thanks to Hershey's chocolate, Mr. Goodbar, Krackel bars, and of course, the ever-popular Hershey's Kisses.

He built a monument to himself in a town he called Hershey in Pennsylvania, home of the Hershey chocolate factory, where his workers could live cheap and enjoy the good life in the Hershey amusement parks, theaters, lakes, zoos, golf courses, and bakeries.

Hershey was a happy town where streets were named after chocolate and the air was filled with the sweet aroma of cocoa. But by 1908, after trying in vain with his wife to have children, and after realizing that he was making more money than he possibly knew what to do with, Hershey decided to endow a school for orphan boys.

Of course, for his gift, Hershey also got something in return: free labor from his boys. The kids had to milk eight hundred cows every morning, helping to produce the one million gallons of daily milk he needed for his chocolate. He rationalized the workload by explaining that the milking helped teach useful skills for the boys. "We do not plan to turn out a race of professors," he said.

Hershey retired in the early 1940s. With his name synonymous with chocolate, he made a decision that seems almost unthinkable today. He gave away the entire $60-million firm—which not only included the chocolate factory, but his theme park, hotels and land as well—to the orphanage.

This meant that every dime spent for a Hershey bar was actually a donation to help educate an orphan child. Eventually, the directors of the trust company split off a chunk for Wall Street, but even today, more than 60 percent of the monies spent on Hershey bars still go to the school.

Hershey not only went down in history for creating an American institution, but his gifts continue to do good, year after year.

ROSEANNE ARNOLD: TURNING NEGATIVES INTO POSITIVES

Roseanne Arnold, the star of ABC's *Roseanne*, has seemed to be able to take negative publicity and make a positive career out of it. I don't believe that she'd be the celebrity she is today if she hadn't surrounded her career with lots of outrageous behavior, which seems to come naturally for her.

Her career has been built on a constant stream of negative stories—be it her gestures while singing the national anthem, her war with certain members of the media, the parking spot incident with Seinfeld's Julia Louis-Dreyfus, the battle with ABC for the renewal of husband, Tom's series, and her alleged abuse as a child.

She's carved her own niche in the entertainment field by being a consistently combative provocateur, but it would all be meaningless if not for the quality of her comedic talent and the success of her TV show. She has a solid base from which she's operating. This has allowed her to turn negatives into positive career enhancement.

JIMMY CARTER: COMBINING HONESTY AND TIMING

In running for president in 1976, the former peanut farmer and Georgia governor chose the best time in history to try for the nation's highest office. A time when being honest was the perfect thing to do. Four years earlier it wouldn't have meant anything, and four years later it didn't mean anything.

But in 1976, after the lies and dishonesty of the Nixon administration, Jimmy Carter, with his choirboy approach to politics and his public pledge to always tell the truth, proved to be good business.

Whether he always told the truth or didn't tell the truth is something for the historians to decide, but the fact is that people believed he was honest about wanting to tell the truth.

When *Playboy* magazine asked him if he had ever desired another woman besides his wife, he seemed to live up to his pledge of being honest. Instead of sidestepping the question—as every other politician would have done—he didn't. He said he had lusted in his heart. The honesty of his answer seemed to give credibility to his claims that he wouldn't lie to the public, even though it created considerable material for comedians and late-night hosts.

No one gave Carter a remote chance of winning the Democratic nomination—let alone the presidency. It was thought that a career politician like Rep. Morris Udall, Sen. Frank Church, or Sen. Henry Jackson might be a more likely winner. But Carter had a keen sense of timing, and by focusing his entire campaign on honesty, pulled off one of the greatest upsets in the history of modern politics.

WHATEVER HAPPENED TO LIONEL RICHIE?

Almost anytime I give a speech, or almost anywhere I go, the first question I'm asked is "Whatever happened to Lionel Richie?"

Lionel, of course, retreated substantially from public view after his marriage began to break up, his father passed away, and he developed some throat problems. Although the level of Lionel's talent never changed, the momentum he had in the early eighties was clearly lost by the end of the decade. He did attempt a brief comeback at the beginning of the nineties with a greatest hits album, and some limited touring, but this hasn't seemed to generate a great deal of renewed momentum.

One day my coauthor said to me: "Ken, if Lionel Richie came back to you, how would you get him back on top?"

Lionel isn't asking, but having given it some thought, the first thing I'd do would be to try and get up to date with his current needs and desires for his life. But since I don't have that luxury, let's just talk about the kinds of career moves that I think could put Lionel back on top.

Perhaps by the time you read this book he may have proved me wrong, but I don't believe the marketplace is such today that Lionel can simply come back with a new album and regain his stature as one of pop music's preeminent superstars.

To make a comeback, Lionel needs to do something different to recapture the public's imagination. Some possibilities:

- Making his acting debut in a major motion picture, while also writing the musical score.

- Singing an unexpected duet with one of today's hottest singers, like Janet Jackson, Garth Brooks, or Billy Joel.

- An all-star tribute album, similar to the recent record of Elton John and Bernie Taupin compositions, sung by such singers as Rod Stewart, Eric Clapton, Jon Bon Jovi, and George Michael. It would give Lionel's songs a new credibility to a younger generation; and with his incredible songs, which include "Three Times a Lady," "Stuck on You" and "Hello," finding material would be no problem.

- Writing a musical for Broadway and/or starring in one.

- Putting a major tour together, investing substantially in sets and staging to deliver the equivalent of the kinds of shows he performed in the early eighties. These were known for their state-of-the-art technology and total excitement. Neil Diamond has clearly shown that current hits are not necessary for touring success when one has a body of exceptional work and outstanding showmanship.

THE COUNTRY EXPLOSION

As far as trends go, I have been very fortunate. In the nineties, country music has been very hot and I've got three terrific country music acts. As Barbara Mandrell said, "I was country before country was cool" and it's the truth. I've been involved with country music since 1976, and in fact, have served as the president of both the Nashville-based Country Music Association (1981) and the West Coast-based president of the Academy of Country Music (1993–95.)

Country is a lot of fun. It's a smaller universe, and there's a great friendliness among the players, the pace is slightly slower, there's an enormous esprit among the business people involved, and a lot of cooperation. Nashville has a true community sense to it, and the techniques that I brought to country from all my years in the pop world have been (at least initially) somewhat unique.

I was fortunate to ride the first big country music explosion in the late 1970s and early 1980s with Kenny Rogers, who, along with Dolly Parton and Willie Nelson, led the surge of country music out of Nashville and onto the pop charts with songs like "The Gambler," "Mamas Don't Let Your Babies Grow Up to Be Cowboys," and "Islands in the Stream."

It's rare when you get an opportunity to ride the same wave twice, but I've been there again in the 1990s with Travis Tritt and Trisha Yearwood, as country once again became the dominant force on the American music scene. There is, however, a significant difference between these two surges.

In the late 70s, country was fueled by artists crossing over onto the pop charts, as well as the movie *Urban Cowboy*, which in fact became the generic title for this new interest in country music. In the nineties, however, it has been the audience that has crossed over, not the artist, as literally millions of people have found themselves alienated or at least disinterested in the directions pop music has taken (i.e., rap and hard rock).

The new country has become more in-tune with the rock of the seventies, upbeat, danceable songs and tunes. With the new wave of country artists—Garth Brooks, Billy Ray Cyrus, Alan Jackson, Dwight Yoakum, Travis Tritt, Wynonna Judd, Trisha Yearwood, and Vince Gill—you're seeing a new kind of country act, artists who are heavily influenced by rock and roll acts and youthful rebellion.

The interesting thing about the new country movement is that it's happened with virtually not one drop of radio airplay on pop stations. One of the great things about country radio was always the loyalty of the audience. Once you succeeded, you could sustain yourself for years. But once country got more popular, the stations suddenly developed the programming habits of pop stations, in the sense that you're only as good as your last record. Regardless of how big an artist you are and how long you've been around, you're not likely to get airplay anymore if you predate Randy Travis.

That makes it frustrating for artists like Kenny Rogers, Willie Nelson, and George Jones, who continue to record excellent material but find it almost impossible to get the records played. Luckily, the fan base is still there, so these artists just have to look at the other areas, such as touring and acting, to reach them.

KENNY, TRAVIS, AND TRISHA— STEP BY STEP

Let's now discuss how I took three virtual unknowns—Kenny Rogers, Travis Tritt, and Trisha Yearwood—and helped them become stars.

We'll begin with Travis, who, as we discussed earlier, was discovered by Danny Davenport, a Warner Bros. Records executive, and brought to me by Nick Hunter, the then head of promotion for the Warner's country label.

Here's the seven-step program I put together after signing on to be Travis's manager.

1. We decided that Travis's three most valuable assets initially were these: live performances, his enormous personal charm, and the involvement of several important people on his team, which gave his career credibility.

2. What I had to do at radio and retail was to create excitement about Travis. To do this, I first had to get all of the people at

Warner Bros. as excited about him as Danny, Nick Hunter, and I were. The Warner field staff's enthusiasm was clearly a key to success.

3. I signed up the best professionals in the business to work for Travis: Randy Travis's publicist; the William Morris Agency to book dates, a top business manager, and a renowned attorney. That was a signal to others that Travis was a major industry player. I also put together an industry showcase for the power brokers in Nashville. Travis's performance that night got everybody in town talking about him.

4. Next, we borrowed $100,000 from Brian Williams at the Third National Bank of Nashville. I had to cosign to get Travis the loan, something I've never done with any other artist. But by now, my belief in Travis was so strong that I didn't consider it to be any real risk. With this money, we bought Randy Travis's old concession bus, so Travis Tritt and his band could get out on the road. Since performing was his greatest asset, I knew that once people saw him, they would become fans and go out and buy his record.

5. Even on those few occasions when Warner Bros. wouldn't put out all the money, we footed the bill to send Travis to visit radio stations. Working closely with the Warner Bros. promotion staff, I also used my own clout to convince stations that Travis was somebody they ought to be playing. I'd had many clients, but most were fully established by the time I got them. And I used that as my theme. I wrote letters to the stations, telling them that Travis was the first new artist I'd signed in twenty years, and the reason was that this guy was something special. I also promised them that when Travis was a star, we would make every reasonable effort to do whatever they needed if they would help us now. What I was asking for, obviously, was an exchange of favors. Fortunately, my promise had some credibility because of my track record turning people into important stars.

6. Travis's first single, "Country Club," sold 92,000 copies and reached number eight on the country charts. Warner Bros. was now really hooked. Their objective became getting the follow-up single, "Help Me Hold On," go all the way to

number one. We stepped up the letter and phone campaigns, and in tandem with Warner's, I worked the radio and retail gatekeepers in every way that I could.

7. We began to broaden Travis's exposure by getting videos on CMT and TNN, appearances on the American Music Awards, the Academy of Country Music award show, and even the Grammys. He played special engagements in important clubs in key cities across the country, such as the Roxy in Los Angeles. He also began to do listener-appreciation shows for various radio stations that had been helpful to him. With four hit singles, the "Country Club" album eventually went platinum and Travis Tritt's career was well on its way.

In summary, we recognized that the key to jump-starting Travis's career was radio airplay and distribution in record stores, and this is what we focused on. We analyzed all of our potential assets, not just Travis's but mine and Warner Bros. as well. We asked, "What will make the gatekeepers say yes?"

The days of payola are fortunately gone, but we realized that we still had something that would motivate radio and retail to help Travis become successful. This was a simple thing called goodwill. It's a perfectly legitimate, legal thing that's done in business every day. We bartered favors. We said, "Help us now, when we need you, and we'll help you later when we're more important and you need us."

The key here was determining what the other parties' needs might be and convincing them that we would, in fact, return the favor.

KENNY ROGERS

I first found Kenny Rogers on the stage of a now-defunct Los Angeles club called Leadbetters. At the time, he was the bass player for a folk-pop group called The First Edition, whose members had broken away from the New Christy Minstrels to form a contemporary group. Kenny was at least ten years older than the rest of the band members, and he was trying his damndest to fit in. He wore long hair, an earring, and dark rose-tinted glasses. He stuck mostly to the background and played bass, while most eyes settled on The First Edition's stunning lead singer, Thelma Camacho.

I was managing the Smothers brothers and producing their TV variety series at the time, and was knocked out by the Edition's sound. I felt there was real hit potential there and signed on as their manager. We booked them to be on the Smothers show the following week. That TV exposure helped them get concert dates, but tensions soon began to flare up.

Kenny was having domestic problems at home, and his status in the group was put into jeopardy. The other members of the group came to me and asked me to lay down the law to Kenny: If he didn't keep his home problems from spilling over into the group, they would have to replace him. Imagine what his history and mine would have been like had this happened. It's funny how close we come sometimes to decisions that can change our lives.

Kenny smoothed things out, and within a year, The First Edition had their first hit, "I Just Dropped In to See What Condition My Condition Was In." More hits followed, and soon we had a situation where one song was climbing the chart, and the record company wanted to put out another single; the problem was they thought the second release might confuse the public. Someone suggested calling the group "Kenny Rogers and The First Edition," on the second release, since Kenny had been singing most of the hits.

It made sense. Kenny had the voice that was dominating the group's sound. It was hard to identify with groups of the day like the Fifth Dimension. It was easier to focus on a name than a group. Initially, the other members of The First Edition weren't too keen on my proposal, but they eventually went along with it, and that second single, "Ruby, Don't Send Your Love to Town," became The First Edition's biggest hit.

Later, after some lean years, The First Edition disbanded in 1975, leaving Kenny $65,000 in debt. He had no plans to go out on his own, until he was approached by a Nashville producer who offered him a $750,000 advance to act as his agent-manager. Kenny saw a way to get out of his financial troubles and moved to Nashville. Unfortunately, the only part of the three quarters of a million he ever saw was $10,000.

Still, our temporary split up wasn't a total negative. It produced a major opportunity. By moving to Nashville, Kenny redirected his career and found country music. By the time I hooked up with Kenny again, about six months later, he had sent me seventeen songs that he was considering for a new album. One of them was "Lucille," the record that—along with his date at the Golden Nugget and well-timed appearance on *The Tonight Show*—put Kenny back on top.

At that time in the mid-seventies, country music looked like the right place to be, and there was a great market for it. Kenny, Dolly Parton, and Willie Nelson became the hot stars of country; Kenny essentially was the Garth Brooks of that era; for a time, he was the biggest-selling recording act in the country.

Kenny's career probably reached its highest point somewhere in the 1980s, but that hasn't stopped him from continuing as one of the industry's highest grossing performers and enjoying a career others would kill for.

Think again about the small plane theory: when a career gets to a certain height, the glide is so long that even if you did nothing to give it any additional energy along the way, you probably wouldn't hit the ground in your lifetime.

If Kenny never did another thing, he could still live and work out his career at a high level. But on the other hand, neither he nor I sit still. We're constantly doing things to keep that flight pattern from eroding. We're giving it bursts of energy—TV work, charity appearances, new albums, concerts, photography projects, restaurants—Kenny is always finding things to keep him interested and excited.

What can we learn from Kenny's career? Be yourself, be diverse, and don't be afraid to work very hard. Kenny has succeeded the most when he was just being honest and being himself. He's funny, charming, and real, and people connect to that. Kenny developed a career with lots of versatility—he has never been static. He became an actor, published books of his photography, opened a chain of chicken restaurants. He works hard to be good at whatever he does, and has an enormous ability to deliver when it really counts.

TRISHA YEARWOOD

The first time I had contact with Trisha Yearwood, I didn't actually meet her. She and her producer Garth Fundis came to an eight-hour career seminar I was giving in Nashville, in the spring of 1991. There, I laid out my entire management philosophy, much of which forms the cornerstone for this book.

Trisha took extensive notes, and went back into the studio to finish her first MCA album, and prepare for her first tour, in support of Garth Brooks.

Trisha was managed at the time by Garth's excellent management team of Pam Lewis and Bob Doyle. Unfortunately, for a variety of reasons, Trisha's arrangement with Doyle and Lewis wasn't working. So the week before the yearly Country Music Association awards show in Nashville, Trisha shocked a lot of people by deciding to part ways with her managers.

When I arrived in Nashville for the show, everyone was talking about what a mistake Trisha was making. The comments ranged from "She's committing career-a-cide" to "She just shot herself in the foot."

We met for a fleeting moment backstage at the CMA show, but the subject of management didn't come up. Then, the day after I returned home, I received a call from Trisha's lawyer, Malcolm Mims, asking if I might be interested in managing Trisha. Almost immediately thereafter, Bruce Hinton, the president of RCA Records, Nashville, called to pose the same question.

I said I was flattered and would think about it. In truth, I knew little about Trisha, other than the fact that she had the year's biggest single, "She's in Love with the Boy." So I picked up the phone and called a number of my friends in Nashville, including record company presidents, agents, and publicists, to ask their opinion. To a person, they all said I'd be crazy not to sign her, that Trisha was clearly destined to be the next star on the Nashville scene.

Buoyed by everyone else's enthusiasm, I called back to say I would take on the job.

We met in Los Angeles, and as with all of my clients, I asked Trisha to create her own balance sheet of assets and liabilities, as well as take a good look at what she wanted out of her life.

I felt that her stunning looks, artistic integrity, and unique voice would be our selling points. I also noticed that she constantly credited Linda Ronstadt as one of her strong influences. It seemed to me that the best way to describe Trisha was to say that she had the potential to be the Linda Ronstadt of the nineties. That became our hook.

Perhaps it would be interesting for you to see the list I made of things to discuss with Trisha before that first face-to-face meeting, as well as the points of the memo I sent to her afterward.

THE LIST

1. Likes, dislikes, goals
2. Background (family, etc.)
3. Hobbies, other interests
4. Financial situation
5. Physical health, weight, exercise
6. Career priorities
   a. *Live show*
   b. *Next album*
   c. *TV exposure*
   d. *Academy of Country Music Awards*
   e. *Horizon Award (CMA)*
   f. *1992 Touring (with whom, how much?)*
   g. *Image Development—build on what you are*
   h. *Photos, press kits*
7. Other things for discussion:
   a. *Christmas gifts/thank yous for MCA staff, radio, agency, etc.*
   b. *Hiring outside publicist*
   c. *Career advertising/budget/reinvest in career*
   d. *Wardrobe*
   e. *Videos (budgets, directors, long form, etc.)*
   f. *Crossing over to Adult Contemporary?*
   g. *Acting interest?*
   h. *Garth Fundis* (her producer)
   i. *Agency relationship*
   j. *Fan fair/radio seminar/other events*
8. Our Relationship
   a. *Honesty!*
   b. *Creativity vs. constant handholding*
   c. *15% commission/no contract/partnership*
   d. *Travel and other expenses*

THE MEMO

What follows are the highlights of a seventeen-page memo I sent to Trisha, outlining our game plan for our first year together.

To: Trisha Yearwood
From: Ken Kragen
Date: 10/25/91
Subject: Meeting Recap and career outline

Trisha, perhaps the most significant moment in our two days together in Los Angeles came when [MCA Records chief] Al Teller asked me to put my thoughts about your career image into just one sentence. As you'll recall, my response was "Trisha Yearwood should be seen as a great singer who also is the most stunningly beautiful woman in country music." I think that thought goes a long way toward defining our game plan. Here, then, are your career priorities.

1. *Get into the very best possible physical shape through proper eating and regular exercise.* To this end we must immediately find a nutritionist and/or trainer to work with you. It is possible we will want to have such a person go on the road with you as well. Getting into shape will not only make you look better, but will make it easier for you to handle the strenuous demands of life on the road.
2. *Improve the quality and excitement of your concert performance.* I will be bringing Joe Layton to one of your shows. Joe has directed numerous Broadway shows (*Annie, Barnum*, etc.) and designed concert acts for dozens of artists (Lionel Richie, Diana Ross, Barbra Streisand, Kenny Rogers and Dolly Parton, Ann-Margret). He is expensive ($50,000 for a typical job) but worth every penny.
3. *Promoting the current album and the singles being released from it is a very high priority.* You must prove that you are not simply a one-hit wonder and that there is a solid career potential here. That is why I put so much emphasis on seeing that the current single goes to No. 1.
4. *A successful career is really a result of the collective efforts of a great number of people* (record promotion men and women, salespeople, booking agents, publicists, managers, lawyers, business managers, promoters and their substantial staffs). All of these people have various priorities in their lives and an important part of our job is to keep you at or near

the top of their lists. One of the best ways to do this is through regular, imaginative, and personalized "Thank yous."

5. *The quality of your next album should be a very high priority.* As Garth Brooks and Travis Tritt have recently proven, it is the *second* album which is the key to a long-term and successful career. You must come back with a second album which is better, more imaginative, and even more commercial than the first.

7. *We are going to need to begin very soon to work on your nomination for awards during the year.* Such nominations are critical because they bring with them potential exposure on the awards show, media attention, and a hook around which we and MCA can do advertising and various other promotions. Ultimately, our goal is the *Horizon Award* for you next year, as well as nominations in the female vocalist, single, album, and video categories.

In the meantime, there are several other award situations to be worked on: The American Music Awards (Monday, 1/27), The Grammy Awards (Tuesday, 2/25), The People's Choice Awards (March), The Academy Awards (to possibly sing a nominated song, as Reba McEntire did this year), The Academy of Country Music Awards (Wednesday, 4/29) and The Music City News Awards (Monday, 6/8). The dates for these award shows need to be blocked on your schedule so that we are sure you are available to do these shows if I am able to get them for you. Moreover, we need to begin immediately to lay out an advertising and promotion campaign geared toward you being nominated and ultimately winning some of these key awards.

8. *New photos are an absolute must.* I have yet to see a photo of you that truly does you justice. You are frankly more attractive in person than your photographs show. We need to engage two or three of the top photographers in order to get some really outstanding photos of you for use in publicity, merchandising, and recorded product.

Trisha, the above encompasses only a portion of what we talked about this week. It is important for you to recognize that it will take a certain amount of time for me to get a good feeling for your abilities and full potential. I find it takes anywhere from a minimum of one month to several for me to understand fully a person's needs, desires, and capabilities. In all of the successful relationships I've had, there is a point along the way when I seem to have a creative breakthrough which allows me to truly map a career plan and direction which will work. What you have before you is a result of my initial impressions and our talks. There will be much more to come in the future. I'm honored to be representing you and looking forward to a long and fruitful relationship.

KK:lha

Nowadays, Trisha and I often look back at that memo with pride, realizing that almost everything in it was, in fact, accomplished.

WRAPPING IT UP: WHERE DO YOU GO FROM HERE?

It's the job that's never started
that takes longest to finish.

—J.R.R. TOLKIEN

Charles William Elliot, the president of Harvard in the late 1800s, was once honored for achieving tremendous success at the university. "Since you became president here," said one speaker, "Harvard has become a storehouse of knowledge."

Responded Elliot: "What you say is true. Harvard is a storehouse of knowledge. But I'm afraid that I can take little credit for this. You see, it is simply that the freshmen bring so much and the seniors take so little away."

I sincerely hope that over these pages I've given you something to take away.

To really benefit from this book, you need to be willing to change the way you look at your life and career. As I have said, your career is *not* your life. It's simply one tool you use to lead a better life.

The principles discussed in *Life Is a Contact Sport* really do work. Just ask Kenny Rogers, the Smothers brothers, Travis Tritt, Trisha Yearwood, Lionel Richie, and other past and present clients. They work for any career. Advancing a career to another plateau, the use of honesty, value of optimism, making contacts—none of these things are limited in any way to just the entertainment field. They'll work for you if you make the effort to understand and apply them.

If you are already doing a lot of the things I've mentioned, congratulations! I hope you'll continue using them, and that you picked up a few new additional ideas that will enable you to have even more success. But let's assume that this approach is somewhat different for you. Let's take a moment to quickly review the principles, and how you can use them for a better life and career:

• The Event Strategy:
The key theorem that has worked for so many of my clients can work for you as well. Just visualize your career as a series of higher and higher plateaus and make upward jumps based on concentrating several events in a very short period of time.

• Creating a Personal Balance Sheet:
You can utilize your assets and eliminate your liabilities on a personal balance sheet. In turn, it will lead to a much better understanding of what you want to do with your life and career.

• Backward Thinking for Forward Motion:
With backward thinking, you can figure out how to get the "gatekeepers" to say yes and let you through.

• Your Life Is Not Your Career:
Your career is simply a tool you use to lead a better life. Make the job work for you and have a great time there; you're much more likely to advance if you're enjoying yourself.

• Optimism and Enthusiasm:
Don't forget that even negatives can be turned into positives, and that people like to be around enthusiastic folks.

• Life Is a Contact Sport:
It's a lot easier than most people think to develop a network of contacts. You already have many valuable connections. As that ad said, "Just do it!"

• Everything in Life Is an Opportunity:
Almost anything that happens in our lives and careers is an opportunity for advancement and success. Train yourself to believe everything happens for a good reason and you'll be amazed how successful you'll become.

• Absolute Honesty Is the Best Gimmick:
Business will beat a path to your door when you establish a reputation for being the most honest person around. Learn to be honest in everything you do.

• Timing Is Everything:
Don't forget that you can do the best work in the world, but if the timing isn't right, it's going to be wasted. Timing is critical.

• The Power of Giving:
You can really enhance your life and career by giving to others. The Power of Giving can bring you the greatest rewards in life, not just spiritually, but emotionally and materially as well. Please do it. You'll be glad you did.

HOUSEPAINTER TIPS

In a way, it was a housepainter who got me into the concept of teaching what I do for others (remember the *Entertainment Tonight* interview?), so I think it's appropriate to close the book with a housepainter. Just remember that you really don't have to be a superstar or a housepainter to use this advice. My ten-step program is viable whether you're baking bread or selling real estate—you just have to adapt these principles to your particular career. The size and shape of the events may differ, depending on whether you're trying to get more customers into your store or making an advertising presentation to a major client, but the concept of big events and multiple impressions still will work just as effectively for you.

But since I told *Entertainment Tonight* that my strategies could work the same magic with a housepainter from Des Moines as with the next Kenny Rogers, let me offer some advice for that midwestern brush-wielding man or woman.

- Networking is critical. It's how you get more work. Every job is a potential reference down the line that can help you land bigger projects. Let's say, for instance, that you're hoping to land a contract to paint the new downtown Hyatt hotel. Begin by thinking backward, and trying to determine who is going to make the decision to hand out the job. Then pursue every possible contact to get directly to that person. Start searching through your list of acquaintances, friends, former employers, relatives, anyone who might have a conduit to that particular decision maker. Most people, when you ask them if they know anybody, will say no, but if you really push them, they'll often come up with someone. Or at least someone who knows someone who knows someone. If you start reaching out far enough, the world's a lot smaller than you think. And the next thing you know, you'll have several people you can call on to help get you that job. Next, you want to learn as much as you can about how that particular "gatekeeper" will make the decision? What are the factors that he or she will be influenced by? Then look at your own assets and find where you can draw on them to help get a decision in your favor. Also look at your liabilities and see if any of them will potentially work against you. If so, make plans to eliminate them, improve them, or minimize their impact.

- In a business like housepainting, I'm sure direct referrals are a large part of anyone's success. You need to impress the clients you already have, and to get from them written letters of recommendation and photos of the job that you can show to new prospects. Then look around for a high-profile job, one that could get you more visibility in the community, like painting the town hall or mayor's office, or offer to paint the local homeless shelter for free.

- Remember how I say that everything in life is an opportunity? Even the job where everything goes wrong can afford you an opportunity. You can show that you're willing to take responsibility for what you do, that you care about the problems that have taken place, and are willing to take measures to correct them. This will enhance your reputation with the customer.

- People enjoy working with optimistic and enthusiastic people. As a housepainter, you're far more likely to be successful if you approach every client in a positive manner and are enthusiastic about what you do and the quality of your work. Your customers will appreciate it, and it will color the way they look at the work you've done. Even somewhat average work may be perceived as better if your customers enjoy having you around.

• Timing is a key career tool for the housepainter. Impress your clients by setting a time which you know you can beat and come ahead of it. Having the job done when you say it's going to be is what your customer (unless she's Murphy Brown) expects of you.

• In a service business like housepainting, it's really important to develop a reputation for honesty. If you promise to have a job done by a certain date, do it. If something happens, don't try to cover up the problem. Earn your client's trust and establish your credibility by being honest about things that don't seem outwardly in your best interest. For instance, don't mask things they'll discover later, but talk to them about the realities of the situation. This will build their confidence in you early on, and help prevent surprise problems down the line.

• Good publicity can really make a difference for a small business. I would begin by examining the kinds of jobs you have done to see if there's anything special about any of them, individually or collectively. If there's nothing unique about them, house by house, then maybe you've painted 150 houses in the last two years and set some sort of a record. You should try to do some jobs that would create stories, such as painting a historic landmark house. Painting an entire street of houses in an unusual color, like pink or purple, or something else along those lines that would be the sort of stunt that would make a fun feature for the Saturday edition and local TV news. Using new, exciting painting technology or old, highly creative work techniques could also be an angle for a story.

I've used these housepainter tips as an example for you, the reader, to see how the concepts of this book can be applied to any life or career no matter how far removed from show business it is. And here are four last general tips before we say goodbye:

• Write It Down:
Whether you're putting a list of assets and liabilities together or thinking backward, the more thoroughly you write it down, the more likely you are to have a road map to follow through on.

• Be Honest with Everybody, Especially Yourself:
This is particularly relevant when you're making a list of your likes
and dislikes, and your assets and liabilities. If you're not sure about
your major assets or liabilities, ask your friends or coworkers. They
often have a better handle on you than yourself.

• Practice:
You can't be good at anything unless you practice all the time. Sports
stars practice things over and over until these things become routine
in their mind. The same principles apply to thinking about the use
of events in your career and being honest in everything you do. The
more you use it, the more natural it becomes.

• Remember, Above All Else, That Life Is a Contact Sport:
Don't forget that the secretary you're nice to today could be running
the company a few years from now.

Thanks for joining me for *Life Is a Contact Sport*. I wish you the best
of luck in your life and career and trust you'll use every opportunity in
your life to build a foundation for success and enjoyment.

Speaking of opportunities, my family and I were on an airplane
returning from New York, and sitting across the aisle from us was the
talented comedian-ventriloquist Ronn Lucas. Ronn had attended my
UCLA extension course, and he told me that after the first session,
he took the principles I'd outlined, went out the next day and booked
$90,000 worth of additional work. Additionally, he told me the insights
he had gained opened up a whole new way for him to view his life
and his career's relationship to it.

A few days later, I was in the process of preparing a video for the
lecture market. So I called Ronn and asked him to bring over one of
his marvelous characters—a dragon named Scorch—to help me make
the tape and he readily said yes. This tape went on to earn me tens
of thousands of dollars in lecture business. And that evening, Ronn
even came over with Scorch to my house and entertained my young
daughter. Now I'm trying to personally advise Ronn with some aspects
of his career.

I tell you this story because it illustrates a number of things I've
talked about in this book. First and most important, that life clearly
is a contact sport. I could fill an entire chapter with the contacts I've
made on airplanes and the opportunities they have led to. Next, the

principle of the power of giving certainly is illustrated here. I gave to Ronn through my teaching at UCLA, he gave back to me by freely appearing on my video, and now, once again, I'm giving back to him with advice on his career. The concept of investing in yourself is here too, for Ronn invested both time and money in attending my UCLA class, and it paid off immediately to the tune of $90,000! I invested in a video to obtain speaking engagements, and it paid for itself in a matter of weeks. And the list goes on and on.

I hope you will all make up those lists of like and dislikes, strengths and weaknesses, goals and objectives, gatekeepers and the influences on their decisions—that you'll view everything in your life (even the most difficult things) as opportunities for growth, learning, and advancement.

The whole point is that *anyone* can be a star in their own career. You don't have to be in the entertainment business to be a star. You can be a star accountant, a star salesman, a star manager in a plant, a star performer in a sales organization. There are stars in every business, and you can be a star in yours. The bottom line is to be the master of your own destiny—setting goals and executing plans to get to those goals.

I work with people all the time who are used to what a standing ovation feels like. But for the corporate executive or blue collar worker, the standing ovation comes from within. It's that moment when you can say, "I did it. I made it happen."

Well, I've done it and the people that I work with have done it. Anyone with a good plan who executes it properly can make it happen too. I hope you'll use the concept of bringing various events together in a concentrated period of time to move to new plateaus, and that you'll seriously consider devoting a portion of your time to giving meaningfully to others. And that, most important, you'll be honest with everyone—including yourself. I guarantee that these things will lead you to a richer and more rewarding life.